Gaines Frank Henry

Bible Course: Outline and Notes

Creation to the Kingdom

Gaines Frank Henry

Bible Course: Outline and Notes
Creation to the Kingdom

ISBN/EAN: 9783337135492

Printed in Europe, USA, Canada, Australia, Japan

Cover: Foto ©Andreas Hilbeck / pixelio.de

More available books at **www.hansebooks.com**

BIBLE COURSE:

OUTLINE AND NOTES.

BY

REV. F. H. GAINES, A.B.

I. Creation to the Kingdom.

ATLANTA, GA.:
FRANKLIN PRINTING AND PUBLISHING CO.
(Geo. W. Harrison, Manager.)
1895.

Entered according to Act of Congress, in the year 1895, by
F. H. GAINES,
In the Office of the Librarian of Congress at Washington.

PREFACE.

The Bible is used as a text-book in a number of the leading institutions of the country. Its claims to a place in the college curriculum are vindicated by the following arguments:

1. *Its adaptation to promote mental development.* The Bible presents to us the greatest subjects in all the range of human thought; such subjects as GOD, CREATION, PROVIDENCE, the MORAL LAW, REDEMPTION, HUMAN RESPONSIBILITY AND DESTINY. And these great subjects are presented and treated by the infinite God himself through inspired men. Where can we find such great subjects presented by such a Teacher?

2. *The great and fundamental value of the knowledge which the Bible alone can impart.* In the department of History the Bible alone gives reliable information concerning the origin of the universe, and of man, concerning the fall, the flood, and the plan of salvation, and indeed is the only authentic history of the world before the flood. In the department of Biography it contains the names of the men who have done more for the human race than all other men. In the departments of Ethnology, of Law, of Psychology the Bible is fundamental. Now add this other most important truth: The Bible alone can furnish the criteria by which the student may judge between the true and the false in philosophy.

3. *The pre-eminent literary value of the Bible.* The Bible itself contains a rich, varied, and peerless literature. For power of thought, for simplicity and perspicuity of style, for force of expression, for poetic beauty and ornate imagery, it stands alone. Moreover, it has directly pro-

duced a vast amount of the finest literature in existence, and is so interwoven with other fine literature that the reader cannot understand, much less appreciate, it without a knowledge of the Bible. Should not a book possessing in itself such unequaled literary value, and so related to the finest literature of the ages, have a place in the college curriculum?

4. *The preservation in college-bred men and women of a true and adequate appreciation of the Bible.* The period of college life is one of marvelous development, not only physically but intellectually, as well as in tastes and attainments. Now suppose this development takes place along all other lines except Biblical lines, in all other kinds of knowledge except Biblical knowledge, what will be the result? Obviously this: The man will still have his boyish ideas of the Bible and his boyish knowledge of the Bible, while he has a man's ideas and knowledge of other books. The result will be a lack of interest in, and appreciation of, the Bible, simply because he has outgrown, not the Bible itself, but the shallow and superficial ideas he had of the Bible as a boy. In order then that the college student may continue to have a true and adequate appreciation of the Bible, let it be put in the college course so that during that most critical period of mental development which takes place in college true views of the Bible may be given.

5. *The adaptation of the Bible to form and develop the highest type of moral character.* To mould and perfect moral character is one of the great objects for which the Bible was designed by its Divine Author. To teach the right, to instill the love of the right, and to guide in the right is the most important end to be attained in the education of the young, and for this the Bible is the only infallible text-book. We conclude, therefore, that there are strong and even unanswerable arguments for the introduction of the Bible into the college course.

PREFACE. v

We are next confronted with a question of very great practical importance, viz.: How should the Bible be taught? This book is the author's answer. It may be helpful, however, to mention and briefly explain the principles upon which the book is written. First, That the Bible itself should be the chief text-book; other books being used only as guides and helps in the study of the Word. Second, That the Bible should be studied systematically, according to a plan. The plan adopted in this book is to divide the Bible into periods indicated by the epochs in the history of the Kingdom of God considered as an organized, visible body. Hence the great central point in the plan is the organization of the visible church in the family of Abraham. All which precedes this central point is in the way of preparation for the organization of the visible church, and all that follows is the unfolding and fulfillment of the Abrahamic Covenant, the great charter of the church. To mark and emphasize this great central point in Biblical history the first period is called Ante-Ecclesiastical—*i. e.*, before the *organization* of the visible church, and the second period Post-Ecclesiastical—*i. e.*, after the *organization* of the visible church. The names of the other periods are descriptive. Third, That the Bible should be taught historically, bringing out in order the great facts in the progress and development of the true religion in the world. Fourth, That the Bible should be taught exegetically, applying true methods and sound laws of interpretation to the Bible with a view to ascertaining its meaning. It is not the purpose of this book to deal with the questions presented by the higher criticism; but to enable the students in our institutions of learning and in Bible classes to obtain a clear knowledge of the contents of the Bible and something of its blessed meaning.

The author has sought in the body of the book to make due acknowledgment of all the authorities quoted. The following works, however, he found specially helpful: Sacred History from the Creation to the Giving of the Law; MS. Notes of Lectures, both by E. P. Humphrey, D.D.; Syllabus of Old Testament History, by Ira M. Price, Ph.D. To these authors he is specially indebted.

This book is printed with the hope and prayer that it may be useful in the study of the Bible. That there is yet great room for improvement the author is fully aware; and he invites criticisms and suggestions from Bible students. F. H. GAINES.

DECATUR, GA., August 8, 1895.

BIBLE COURSE: OUTLINE AND NOTES.

SPECIAL INTRODUCTION.

SECTION 1. THE BIBLE.

GENERAL FEATURES.

OUTLINE.

I. **The Names Given to Our Sacred Books.**
Ency. Britannica, art. Bible; Companion to the Bible (Barrow), chap. 13; Bible Dict. (Smith).

II. **The Biblical Development.**
Butler's Bible Work, vol. 1, sec. 2; Sacred Hist. from Creation to the Giving of the Law (Humphrey), chap. 1; Companion to the Bible, chap. 13.

III. **The Canon.**
Bible Dict., Companion to the Bible, pp. 194–196; Outlines of Theology (Hodge), p. 93.

IV. **The Men who Wrote the Bible.**
Outlines of Theology, p. 57; Sacred History from Creation to the Giving of the Law, p. 3.

V. **Inspiration.**
Hodge's Outlines of Theology, p. 70; Evidences of Christianity (Alexander), chap. 14.

VI. **The Books of the Bible.**
Syllabus of Old Testament History (Price), sec. 9, p. 21; cf. Companion to the Bible, chaps. 17–18.

VII. **Period of Old Testament History.**

NOTES.

I. **The Names Given to Our Sacred Books.**
1. *Bible.* The word Bible, "in medieval Latin and in English, treated as a singular noun, is in its original Greek form plural—τὰ βιβλία, the (sacred) books—correctly expressing the fact that the Sacred Writings of Christendom are made up of a number of independent records which set before us the gradual development of the religion of revelation."—*Ency. Britannica.* This name, as applied to the whole collection of sacred books of the Old and New Testaments, can be traced as far back as the fifth century. The name Bible in its application to our sacred books expresses two ideas: (1) The unity of revelation—many books, yet one book. (2) The importance of revelation—this revelation being *the* book (Bible) of all books.

2. *Scripture* (singular and plural). Acts 8:32; 2 Tim. 3:16. The word Scripture is from the Latin *scribo, scribere*, to write. It means primarily anything written, a writing. But by way of eminence or distinction it is applied to the books of the Old and New Testaments. It is at present nearly always used in the last sense, as one of the names of our sacred books. As thus used, it emphasizes the importance of the Bible as being THE Writings—*i. e.*, the Sacred Writings, and hence the most important writings.

3. *The Word of God.* Eph. 6 : 17. This name points to the divine origin of the Bible. It implies that this book is a revelation (word) from God.

NOTE.—These names are descriptive. What kind of a book do they describe? With what frame of mind and heart should we enter upon its study?

II. Biblical Development.

1. *The Bible a Growth.* It grew in process of time in the number of books or documents composing it. At first the five books of Moses were given. Then in the course of centuries other inspired books or writings were added, until finally the whole number reached sixty-six. Then it also grew "in the unfolding of divine truth." "The sacred writers begin by revealing one God, and gradually ascend to the mystery of Three in One; they begin with a lamb slain at the first altar, and rise to the God-man slain for sin, and thence to the Lamb slain enthroned in glory."—*Humphrey.*

2. *Divisions in this Development.*

(1) It is divided into two great periods by the coming of Christ. The books of the Bible belonging to the period before the coming of Christ are called collectively the Old Testament, and that period is designated by the letters B. C. The books of the Bible belonging to the period after the coming of Christ are called collectively the New Testament, and this period is designated by the letters A. D.

(2) The minor divisions in the Old Testament are sometimes twofold (Matt. 11:13), and sometimes threefold. (Luke 24: 44). The

latter division, the more common by the Jews, the *Law* (Pentateuch), *Prophets*, (Joshua, Judges, Samuel, Kings, all together sometimes called Former Prophets. To these were added all the strictly prophetic books except Daniel). The Psalms and writings included all the remaining books of the Old Testament.

III. The Canon.

Definition: "The collection of books which form the original and authoritative written rule of the faith and practice of the Christian Church." —*Bible Dict.*

1. *Canon of Old Testament.* "To Ezra and his coadjutors, the men of the Great Synagogue, the Jews ascribe the completion of the canon of the Old Testament. Respecting the question when the canon of the Old Testament received its finishing stroke, a question which the wisdom of God has left in obscurity, we must speak with diffidence. We know with certainty that our present Hebrew canon is identical with that collection of sacred writings to which our Saviour and his Apostles constantly appealed as invested throughout with divine authority."—*Barrow, Comp. Bible,* 194 *and* 196.

2. *Canon of New Testament.* As commonly received, the canon of the New Testament was ratified by the Council of Carthage, A. D. 397.—*Bible Dict.*

3. *The Difference between Canon of Protestants and Canon of Church of Rome.* In addition to the books of the Protestant canon, Rome adds Tobit, Wisdom, Judith, Ecclesiasticus, Baruch,

and the two books of Maccabees. They also prefix to the book of Daniel the History of Susannah, and insert in the third chapter the Song of the Three Children, and add to the end of the book the History of Bel and the Dragon. Even in the Roman Church their authority was not accepted by the most learned and candid men until it was made an article of faith by the Council of Trent in the sixteenth century.

IV. The Men who Wrote the Bible.

The Bible is a collection of sixty-six books, written by about forty *different men*. "These writers were for the most part strangers each to all the others, separated by habits of life, by degrees of knowledge, by social position, by forms of civilization, and by dividing tongues and more dividing ages. Yet, withal, these books could not have been more thoroughly one in their general plan and method of thought if they had been composed by a single person in a single year of his life. This oneness of plan is not limited to historical statements, but extends to revelations from the spiritual world which are beyond the reach of human discovery or intuition, and upon which the imagination and reason of all other authors have run into confusion."— *Humphrey's Sacred Hist.*, etc., p. 3.

V. The Books of the Bible.

1. *Number of Books in All—Sixty-six.*
   In Old Testament, thirty-nine.
   In New Testament, twenty-seven.
   Name the books of the whole Bible in order.
2. *Kinds of Literature in Old Testament.—Historical, Poetical, Prophetical.*

(1) Historical, seventeen, as follows: Pentateuch, Joshua, Judges, Ruth, 1 and 2 Samuel, 1 and 2 Kings, 1 and 2 Chronicles, Ezra, Nehemiah, and Esther.

(2) Poetical, five, as follows: Job, Psalms, Proverbs, Ecclesiastes, Canticles.

(3) Prophetical, seventeen, as follows: Major Prophets five and Minor Prophets twelve.

VI. Inspiration.

"Inspiration is such a divine influence upon the minds of the sacred writers as rendered them exempt from error, both in regard to their ideas and words."—*A. Alexander.*

This definition applies, of course, to the Scriptures in the original tongue in which they were written. 2 Tim. 3:16; 2 Pet. 1:21.

NOTE.—Importance which this fact gives to the Bible.

VII. Periods of Old Testament History.

First Period—Ante-Ecclesiastical.
From Creation to the call of Abram—2,083 years.*

Second Period—Patriarchal. Post-Ecclesiastical
From the call of Abram to the Exodus—430 years.

Third Period—Wandering.
From the Exodus to settlement in Canaan—91 years.

Fourth Period—Judges.
From settlement in Canaan to the Kingdom—305 years.

---

*Chronology of Usher.

SPECIAL INTRODUCTION. 7

Fifth Period—Kingdom.
From the ascension of Saul to the division of the Kingdom—120 years.
Sixth Period—The Kingdoms of Judah and Israel. Contemporary
From the division of the Kingdom to the fall of the Kingdom of Israel—253 years.
Seventh Period—The Kingdom of Judah. Continued.
From the fall of the Kingdom of Israel to the fall of Jerusalem close of the Old Testament—277 years. 135
Eighth Period — The Exile 70 "
Ninth " — The Restoration -

SECTION 2. THE APOCRYPHA.

OUTLINE.

I. **The Meaning of the Word Apocrypha.**
Schaff-Herzog Ency.; Bible Dict. (Smith); Companion to the Bible, p. 350.

II. **The Apocryphal Books of the Old Testament.**
Bible Dict.; Companion to the Bible, p. 350.

III. **The Apocryphal Books of the New Testament.**
Bible Dict.; Companion to the Bible, p. 517.

IV. **The Value of the Apocrypha.**

NOTES.

I. **The Meaning of the Word Apocrypha.**
The primary meaning of the Greek word Apocrypha is hidden or secret. Applied to writings it describes such as are of unknown origin or authorship. From this primary meaning of the word the transition was easy to the secondary meaning of spurious or false. So the early Christian writers applied the word apocrypha to anonymous or spurious books which falsely laid claim to be a part of the inspired volume.

II. The Apocryphal Books of the Old Testament.

The number varies as given by different authors. Smith's Bible Dictionary gives a list of fourteen; Barrow, in Companion of the Bible, reckons the number as ten. The most important, however, are those in dispute between the Romanists and Protestants. These are six in number, as follows: "Tobit, Judith, Wisdom, Ecclesiasticus, Baruch, and the two books of Maccabees, and also some additional chapters annexed to the book of Esther, which are not in the Hebrew; and to the book of Daniel the History of Susannah and the Song of the Three Children are prefixed, and the History of Bel and the Dragon is annexed. These books and portions of books are likewise placed at the end of the Old Testament in our large English Bibles under the name Apocrypha."—*Alexander.*

III. The Apocryphal Books of the New Testament.

These are very numerous. They may be divided into four groups: 1. Gospels; 2. Acts of the Apostles; 3. Epistles from Apostles; 4. Revelations. But from the very oldest time a suspicion of heresy clung to them all, and contributed much to finally throw the whole literature into the shade. When the canon of the New Testament was fixed, and the Apocryphal books thereby became exiled, they ceased to be read, and in the Middle Ages even their names were forgotten."—*Schaff-Herzog Ency., art. Apocrypha.*

IV. Value.

Concerning the Old Testament Apocrypha Barrow says: "Although the Protestant churches rightly reject the Apocryphal books as not belonging to the inspired word, the knowledge of their contents is nevertheless a matter of deep interest to the biblical scholar." Concerning the New Testament the same author says: "To the student of church history they are not without value; for they illustrate the origin of many ancient traditions and some ritual observances. But if we look to their intrinsic character, they may be described as a mass of worthless legends abounding in absurd and puerile stories."

BIBLE COURSE.

FIRST PERIOD.

ANTE-ECCLESIASTICAL. FROM THE CREATION TO THE CALL OF ABRAHAM, 2,083 YEARS.

Introduction.
The Narrative of Creation.
I. **Characteristics.**
II. **Explanatory.**

NOTES.

I. **Characteristics.**
1. *Conciseness.* What great events are here crowded into a single chapter, even into single verses! Bearing upon interpretation.
2. *The Importance of the Narrative.* Relation to the Bible. Also reveals the relation of God to the universe and to us.
3. *The Style.* For simplicity and perspicuity and grandeur, what in all literature can excel this narrative?

II. **Explanatory.**
1. *A Summary of the Whole.* 1:1–2.
2. *The Creator.* God, not many, but one.
3. *Time.* In the beginning, *i. e.*, at the first, when the universe first began to be.
4. *Meaning of Create.* To originate. This the prerogative of God alone.

5. *What Did God Create?* V. 1, the universe.
6. *The Condition of the Earth Prior to the First Day?* V. 2, "Without form," empty, dark.
 " Vast, immeasurable abyss,
 Outrageous as a sea, dark, wasteful, wild."—*Milton.*
7. "*The Spirit of God.*" This usually understood to be the Third Person in the Trinity. "It signifies the approach of a divine influence to the helpless, lifeless chaos. Order and life comes from God, not from matter.—*Dodd.*"

SECTION 1. THE WEEK OF CREATION.
GEN. 1: 1-31; 2: 1-3.

OUTLINE.

First Day.
Light, 1:3–5. Dabney's Theology, p. 251. Commentaries.

Second Day.
Firmament, vs. 6–8. Dabney's Theology, p. 252. Commentaries.

Third Day.
Gathering together of the waters. Vegetable kingdom, vs. 9–13. Dabney's Theology, as above.

Fourth Day.
Sun, moon, and stars, vs. 14–19. Dabney's Theology.

Fifth Day.
Oviparous animals, 20-23. Dabney's Theology.

Sixth Day.
Higher land animals, and man, 24–31. Syllabus of Old Testament History (Price), p. 24.

FIRST PERIOD. 13

Seventh Day.
Sabbath, 2: 1-3. Sacred History from Creation to the Giving of the Law (Humphrey), p. 47.

Creation as a Whole.
Sacred History, etc. (Humphrey), p. 17.

NOTES.

First Day.
Light. Whence? Some answer that it was cosmic; or the result of the chemical action of the gases. Others agree that we cannot answer until we know more of light. "All the researches of modern optics go more and more to overthrow the belief that light is a substantive emanation from the sun. What it is, whether a substance or an affection of other substances, is still unknown. Hence, it cannot be held unreasonable that it should have existed before the sun; nor that God should have regulated it in alternations of day and night."—*Dabney.*

Second Day. 1:6-8.
Firmament (expanse). "The atmosphere either created or else disengaged from chaos and assigned its place around the surface of the earth. This, by sustaining the clouds, separated the waters from the earth."—*Dabney.*

Third Day. 1:9-13.
"The work of the third day was to separate the terrestrial waters from the dry ground, to assign each their bounds, and to stock the vegetable kingdom with its genera of trees and plants."—*Dabney.*

Fourth Day. 1:14-19.
Creation of sun, moon, and stars, "or else the assignment to their present functions of sun, moon, and stars,

and henceforth these became the chief depositories, or else propagators, of natural light."—*Dabney.*

Fifth Day. 1: 20-23.

"Creation of all oviparous animals, including the three classes of fishes, reptiles, and birds."—*Dabney.* This is the first time God is said to have blessed any of his works of creation (v. 22). Why begin here? These sentient creatures. What was this blessing? Continuance, multiplication (latter part of v. 22). Then doubtless the additional ideas of supplying their wants and of making their existence a pleasure to themselves, so adapting his blessing to the organism and sphere of each as to make the existence of each a pleasure. So it seems, *e. g.*, the singing of the birds would seem to indicate pleasure, also the gambol of lambs. Behold the goodness of God! The blessing afterwards bestowed upon man was something different and higher.

Sixth Day. vs. 24-31.

1. Higher land animals: (*a*) cattle; (*b*) creeping things of the ground. 2. Creation of man: (*a*) God created man in his own image; (*b*) created male and female; (*c*) blessed them; (*d*) commanded, "be fruitful and multiply"; (*e*) have dominion over all creatures; live on vegetation.

Seventh Day. 2: 1-13.

Price: "'This blessing' (upon the animals) 'was not limited to those individual beings which were immediately created by God, but was intended for all the following generations. In like manner the blessing on the first Sabbath indicated that the day down to the end of time was a gift of God to man laden with blessings." God also hallowed the Sabbath, *i. e.*, "consecrated the day to rest from labor, to holy service and worship; setting it apart from all the other days of the week, and thus giving to it a higher significance. The Sabbath is not a holiday, but a holy day." The Sabbath is also a *memorial* of God's great work of creation (see fourth commandment, which is a reënactment of the primeval Sabbath).

Creation as a Whole.
1. It is marked by *unity*. Each day is a preparation and prophecy of some other day. This adaptation or interdependence is shown by a table given by Professor Dana, as follows:

First day—Light created. Fourth day—Luminaries appear.
Second day—Firmament. Fifth day—Air and water peopled.
Third day—Dry land. Sixth day—Animals and man.

"The work of the first, second, and third days was prophetic of the fourth, fifth, and sixth, each to each."—*Humphrey.* Does not this indicate a plan, and hence an intelligent First Cause? And does not the unity of the plan indicate the unity of the Creator?

2. The order of creation climactic.
3. All "good," "very good." v. 31.
4. Blessing upon all sentient creatures.

SECTION 2. MAN.
Gen. 2: 4-25.

OUTLINE.
Introduction.
Subject of this passage, Man.

I. The Peculiarities of Man's Creation.
Humphrey's Sacred Hist., etc., chap. 3.
Price's Syllabus of Old Test. Hist., p. 26.

II. Eden.
Humphrey's Sacred Hist., pp. 44 and 48.
Blaikie's Manual of Bible Hist., p. 17.

III. Woman.
Humphrey's Sacred Hist., p. 32.

IV. The Covenant of Works.
Dabney's Theology, pp. 302–305.

V. The Four Primeval Ordinances.
Humphrey's Sacred Hist., etc., pp. 46–49.

NOTES.

Introduction.

The design of the sacred writer in this passage is not to give a second account of creation, but to describe man, his origin, his relation to the lower creation, his home, his relation to God, and his relation to woman. Hence, the subject of this chapter is Man.

I. The Peculiarities of Man's Creation.

Compare 1:26–27 and 2:7.

"The word 'likeness' explains the word 'image'; that is to say, God made man in an image like himself. This image is not predicated of the body, for God had none," but of the soul. This *likeness* pertains to the soul in the following respects:

1. *The Substance of the Soul:* God a spirit—man's soul spirit.
2. *Intelligence:* God a rational being; so man.
3. *Moral Nature:* God—man (conscience).
4. *Personality:* God a person, a being possessed of intelligence, feeling, free agency; so man.
5. *Free Agency:* God—man.
6. *Affections:* God—man.

7. *Moral Righteousness:* This element of man's likeness to God displays the divine image in its highest glory. "Three sources are open from which we may take knowledge of man's original righteousness. Putting together our best conception of the holiness of God, of the holiness of Christ, of all that is holy in the renewed man, we reach a conception of the original righteousness in which man was created."— *Humphrey.*

8. *Immortality:* God—man.

II. Eden.

1. *What Was Eden?* Eden (delight) was "a garden," a spot specially selected and prepared— prepared *by the Lord God.* In this garden the LORD God made to grow every tree that is pleasant to the sight and good for food. Besides, in the middle of the garden he planted "the tree of life" and "the tree of the knowledge of good and evil." The narrative thus plainly teaches that Eden was a place adapted by the LORD God to meet every want of man and also to his highest enjoyment, thus leaving no excuse for disobedience.

2. *The Location of Eden.* Where was Eden? The three continents of the Old World have been subjected to the most rigorous search; from China to the Canary Islands, from the Mountains of the Moon to the coast of the Baltic, no locality which in the slightest degree corresponds to the description of the first abode of the human race has been left unexamined. The great rivers of Europe, Asia, and Africa have in turn done service as the Pison and

Gihon of Scripture, and there remains nothing but the New World wherein the next adventurous theorist may bewilder himself in the mazes of this most difficult question." "The most prevalent notion, however, has been that the garden lay in the highlands of Armenia, where the Euphrates and the Tigris and two other great rivers, now called the Kizil-Ermock and the Araxes have their rise."—*Blaikie.*

3. *The Employment of Man in Eden.* 2:15. "Labor is not a part of the penalty of sin. While man stood in his innocency 'the Lord took the man and put him into the garden of Eden to dress it and to keep it.' Sin brought a curse upon toil. Labor, before the first sin, was expended upon a garden most kindly and fruitful; toil after that catastrophe was expended on a thorny and reluctant soil; but labor was, as well before sin as after, the appointment of God to man. Labor without irksomeness and slavish toil, which makes acts otherwise tedious a delightful repose; which is itself physical enjoyment and the keenest stimulus and relish of the mind—labor was one of the blessings of paradise."—*Humphrey.*

III. Woman. 2:18-25.

1. *Woman Was Created after Man.* Significance? 1 Tim. 2:13.
2. *The Purpose of Woman's Creation.* To be an help meet for man. 2:18–20; cf. 1 Cor. 11:9.
3. *The Method of Woman's Creation.* 2:21–22. This unique creation yields several important results: (*a*) Clears up the doctrine of

the unity of the race, both in origin and species. The first pair not of different races or of different families of the same race. (*b*) Establishes the indissoluble character of the covenant of marriage. (See Matt. 19 : 6.) Inculcates monogamy—for so undoubtedly it was at the beginning. (*c*) Indicates the love and tender care which should characterize the marriage relation—for husband and wife are one.

IV. The Covenant of Works.

God having created man, as described above, in his own image and placed him in the Garden of Eden, did "enter into a covenant of life with him upon condition of perfect obedience." We come here to the first of a series of covenants described in the Scriptures. But what is a covenant? A covenant, in its more technical sense, implies (1) two equal parties; (2) liberty to do or not to do the covenanted things before the covenant is formed. In this sense there could be no covenant between God and man. But in the more general sense of a conditional promise, such a transaction was evidently effected between God and Adam, and is recorded in Gen. 2: 16–17.—*Dabney*. In the sense thus explained we have here a covenant, an agreement, or contract, between two parties. This covenant is known as the *Covenant of Works*, because the condition of life was the work of perfect obedience.

Analysis of the Covenant of Works.

(1) The parties, God and Adam.
(2) The subject—Adoption. Transferring man from the position of a servant to that of a son, and surrounding him forever with the safe-

guards of the divine wisdom and faithfulness, making his holiness indefectible.—*Dabney, p. 302.*

(3) God's part—To give adoption.
(4) Adam's part—Perfect obedience.
(5) The sanctions—The promise and threat.
(6) The seal—Tree of life, as is commonly supposed.

Explanations of Above.

(1) In this covenant Adam represented himself and his posterity.
(2) The obedience required was perfect obedience, in heart as well as act; obedience to the revealed will of God; moral as well as positive commands.
(3) The life promised eternal life; the death threatened eternal death.
(4) It is also reasonable to infer that a definite (limited) probation was appointed.

This Really a Covenant of Grace.

(*a*) It was an act of grace for God to enter into a covenant with man. (*b*) It was an act of grace to establish him forever in holiness for obedience limited in duration. (*c*) It was an act of grace to allow the *first* man, under the most favorable circumstances, to represent his posterity. (*d*) The promise was most gracious. (*e*) The circumstances under which Adam entered upon his trial most favorable. (*f*) The test simple and easy, as we shall see.

V. The Four Primeval Ordinances.

1. Dominion. 2. The Sabbath. 3. Marriage. 4. Labor. "Now these four ordinances are not accidents in our nature or our position. Neither

of them was an afterthought, nor were they introduced one by one in the lapse of ages into the bosom of the human race. They are not gifts of divine grace imparted to man as a sinner in his sins, or as a sinner saved from his sins. They were granted to man as man in the very beginning. Their necessity is deeply laid in the necessity of his being."—*Humphrey*. What would be the effect upon society if either one of the four should be abolished?

SECTION 3. THE FALL.
GEN. 3.

OUTLINE.

I. **The Test of Man's Obedience.**
Humphrey's Sacred Hist., etc., chap. 4.

II. **The Temptation, 3: 1-6.**
Humphrey's Sacred Hist., etc., chap. 4.
Price's Syl., p. 28.

III. **The Sin whereby Adam Fell.**
Humphrey as above.
Dabney's Theol., p. 310.

IV. **The Fall.**
Humphrey and Dabney, as above.

V. **The Guilty Pair before the Great Judge.**
Humphrey, chap. 4.

VI. **The First Gospel.**
Humphrey's Sacred Hist., etc., chap. 5.

NOTES.

I. The Test of Man's Obedience.

The test of man's obedience under the covenant of works was the forbidden fruit. 2:17. Was this a reasonable and suitable test? The following facts will help us to answer:

(See Humphrey's Sacred Hist., pp. 51–52.)
1. "Adam was a mature man."
2. "He was holy."
3. "He held direct intercourse with God."
4. "He was sufficiently forewarned."
5. "Every lawful enjoyment was offered him."
6. "The duty enjoined was not difficult."
7. "The test was simple and intelligible."

II. The Temptation. vs. 1-6.

1. *The Tempter.* v. 1. Serpent? Devil in form of a serpent. Cf. Rev. 12:9; 20:2. See Price, p. 28, par. 6.
2. *Whom Does the Serpent Address?* v. 2.
3. *The Manner of the Temptation.*
    (1) An adroit insinuation—"*Every tree.*" Did God make *any* prohibition? If so, was it not strange and hard? The insinuation against God. The form of a question.
    (2) The effect upon Eve. vs. 2–3. The insinuation had its desired effect. It gained the attention of Eve. She stopped to listen and parley; she entertained the question. Here her first great blunder. Then she exaggerated the prohibition (see her interpolation), indicating that she *did* think it arbitrary and hard.
    (3) Satan promises safety in sinning. v. 4. He grows bolder. This a direct charge of false-

hood against God. Eve makes no reply. Significance?

(4) Insinuates that God is jealous of their happiness and had on that account kept the truth from them. "For God doth know," etc.

(5) Promises great advantages in sinning. v. 5. Note steps in the temptation.

4. The result. v. 6. Eats. Then gave to her husband.

III. The Sin whereby Adam Fell.

1. *A Sin against God.* Violation of his command.
2. *The Elements of his Sin.* (1) Unbelief, a sin of heart. (2) Disobedience an outward act. Jas. 1:14–15.
3. *The Aggravation of Adam's Sin.* Ingratitude. Knowledge. Against his posterity, etc.
4. *The Difference between the Sin of Adam and Eve* v. 6 (latter part). See also 2 Cor. 11:3; 1 Tim. 2:14. "But these declarations do not prove that Satan alone tempted the woman, and the woman alone tempted the man. The phrase in Genesis must not be overlooked. She gave to her husband *with her*. He was probably present at the time, consenting to what she said and did. She took the lead in the guilty act; she joined her solicitations with the solicitations of the tempter; but the guilt of man and of woman was substantially the same. To the full extent in which he was personally influenced by the Devil, and in which he failed to defend the purity of his wife, he is considered by all good men dishonored and guilty."—*Humphrey, p.* 56.

IV. The Fall.
A figurative use of the word (exp.).
1. *It was Moral*—the loss of original righteousness and the corruption of his whole nature.
2. *It was a Fall in Reference to his Relations with God*—loss of communion with God and of all the privileges of a son of God—spiritual death.
3. *It was Physical*—from perfect health to liability to bodily death.
4. *Liable to Eternal Death.*
5. *The Immediate Effects of the Fall upon Adam and Eve.* (*a*) They suffered under a sense of moral degradation. "Their eyes were opened." (v. 11.) (*b*) They experienced dread of judgment—" hid themselves." (*c*) Became deceitful, shuffling, and insolent. vs. 10–13.
6. *The Effect upon Adam's Posterity.* Rom. 5:12–21. Facts.

V. The Guilty Pair before the Great Judge.
1. *Their Guilt Clearly Established.* vs. 9–13.
2. *Judgment Pronounced*:
    (1) Upon the tempter. vs. 14–15.
    (2) Upon the woman. v. 16.
    (3) Upon the man. vs. 17–19.
3. *The Expulsion.* vs. 22–24.

VI. The First Gospel. v. 15. Protevangelium.
It pleased God to embody in the very bosom of the curse a gleam of hope, thus giving intimation of mercy and judgment. Notice—
1. *This a promise of salvation, accepted as the first Messianic promise.* "This promise comes before us in its germ, to be gradually unfolded through

the ages. The ultimate victory of the kingdom of light over the kingdom of darkness is predicted, and the assurance is added that this victory shall be won by the seed of the woman. But who are to be the seed of the woman? The expression bears a threefold meaning: Primarily, it signifies the whole human family, for Eve is the mother of all living. More precisely, it describes the righteous portion of the race: 'The good seed are the children of the kingdom.' (Matt. 13 : 38.) In its highest sense it is predicated of Christ, who is proved by genealogical tables to be the direct descendant of the first pair."—*Humphrey, p.* 68. Which seed is meant in the promise?

2. *We have here "prophetic" intimations of the plan of salvation.*

(See Humphrey's Sacred Hist., p. 69.)

(1) "Salvation shall come through a person."
(2) "This Saviour shall be a man and yet more than a man."
(3) "The Saviour shall be the seed of the woman severally, not of the man and woman jointly."
(4) "The Redeemer should be a suffering and a triumphant Messiah."
(5) "The salvation purchased for us by the seed of the woman will be complete."
(6) "Redemption was promised not only to the first man and woman, but to their posterity likewise."
(7) "God put enmity between the two seeds." Hence, conflict of the ages.

SECTION 4. THE CAINITES.

GEN. 4.

OUTLINE.

I. Early History of Cain and Abel.
Humphrey's Sacred Hist., chap. 4. Price's Syllabus, pp. 29–30. Geikie's Hours, p. 140.

II. Cain's Great Crime.
Same authorities.

III. Cain before the Great Judge.
Humphrey's Sacred Hist, pp. 87–88.

IV. Cain in the Land of Nod.
Humphrey and Price, as above. Geikie, p. 146.

NOTES.

I. Early History of Cain and Abel.

1. *The Moral Condition in which They were Born.* "A corrupt nature was conveyed from our first parents to their immediate posterity; by the hideous wickedness of Cain we may measure the depth of depravity in the generation next to Adam; the first murder being the natural product of the first transgression." Cf. Ps. 51:5; Job 14:4.

2. *Their Occupations.* 4:2. These occupations "have been called the ground forms of human industry." "No interval of 'utter degeneracy' is sanctioned in the Scripture account of the first man; no dismal age of living on roots and shell fish, or the produce of the chase, or naked savages; they begin in Eden, to work it and

watch it; and after the fall they turn to the tillage of the field, and rearing and tending of sheep, occupations from which an advance to other forms of civilization was easy."—*Geikie.*

3. *Their Religious Principles Held in Common.* Their offerings indicate that they both believed, (1) In the existence of God; (2) In the duty of worshipping him.

4. *The Difference in their Religious Principles.* Heb. 11:4: "Abel had faith, Cain had none; and for this reason Abel's service was 'a more acceptable service than Cain's.' The precise nature and extent of this faith has not been determined. Some of our best interpreters teach us that Abel's faith led him to make a bloody sacrifice for sin, while Cain's unbelief led him to exclude, intentionally perhaps, the idea of propitiation from his offering."—*Humphrey.* Others think the narrative in Genesis 3:21 does not warrant us to conclude that God had appointed bloody sacrifices at this early period.

II. Cain's Great Crime.

1. *The Occasion of the Crime.* The acceptance of Abel's sacrifice and the rejection of his own. 4:3–5.
2. *The Cause of his Crime.* Jealousy. vs. 5–6.
3. *The Crime Itself.* Murder, fratricide. v. 8. First murder.
4. *The Aggravations of his Crime.* (*a*) The expostulation of God. vs. 6–7. (*b*) Premeditation and deceit. v. 8.

III. Cain before the Great Judge.

1. *The Trial.* The judge. The accused. The attitude and conduct of Cain before the LORD.

v. 9. See how sin leads to sin. Found guilty. v. 10.

2. *Sentenced.* vs. 11–12. Elements: (1) "Cursed art thou from the ground." (2) "When thou tillest the ground it shall not yield unto thee her strength." (3) "A fugitive and a wanderer shalt thou be in the earth."

3. *Cain's Response.* "My punishment is greater than I can bear." "My *punishment*"—not my guilt; "the cry of remorse embittered by impenitence and despair." Then follows Cain's lamentation: "I am an exile from home; I am an outcast from the favor and protection of the LORD, and every one that finds me shall slay me. But the LORD answered." v. 15. What this mark was we know not. Why was Cain's life spared?

IV. Cain in the Land of Nod.

1. *Where was the Land of Nod?* The narrative (v. 16) says "on the east of Eden." "The geography of Nod cannot be defined. The name signifies the land of Exile or Flight, contrasting Eden, the land of Delight."

2. *Cain's Wife.* He evidently "took with him one of his sisters as his wife. The marriage between brothers and sisters in this family was plainly unavoidable. These alliances yield one important result. The doctrine of the absolute unity of the race is derived from the creation of one man and the formation of his one wife from his person; and that unity was distinctly maintained by the intermarriage of the sons and daughters of the first pair."

3. *The Building of the First City.* "Cain introduced a new form of society by building a city or fortress." v. 17. This "introduced a new epoch in human history and with it a new civilization."

4. *The Cainite Civilization.* Passing over the uneventful period covered by four generations of Cainites, the historian comes down to Lamech. From this one man and his remarkable family of three sons and one daughter the new civilization received its type.

The Elements of this Civilization.

(1) Polygamy—introduced by Lamech himself; the development of ungodliness, indecency, and incipient heathenism; in marriage dishonored and polluted, and in the degradation of woman.

(2) The pastoral life of the Eastern tribes—introduced by Jabal (Profit).

(3) Music—Tubal. He "invented the harp and organ, stringed and wind instruments, and with them, doubtless, the science and art of music."

(4) Manufactures from the metals—Tubal-Cain. v. 22. "The industries of the three brothers, in the manufacture of musical instruments, tent-making, the working in metals, the production of edge-tools, with the implements of husbandry and war, indicate great progress in mining, smelting, spinning, weaving, and the forging and polishing of brass and iron."— *Humphrey.*

(5) The charms of womanhood—Naamah, the Lovely. v. 22.

5. *Lamech's Song.* vs. 23–24. These verses "shed additional light upon the times. Lamech a murderer, and he exceeded the hardihood of his ancestor, Cain, by an open defiance of justice, human and divine. See his 'Song of the Sword.' This ode, considered as a product of thought, is worthy of attention, because it is the oldest lyrical fragment in all literature, its date being fixed at more than 1,200 years before the deluge. . . . . The import of the song is that Cain was shielded from punishment by the divine protection; Lamech is armed and can take care of himself. God would inflict seven-fold vengeance on the man who should lay hands on Cain; Lamech will retaliate an attack upon him seventy times seven. . . . . Dreschler remarks, 'The history of the Cainites began with a deed of murder and ended with a song of murder.' . . . . The Cainite civilization foreshadowed the civilization of Babylon, of Corinth, of Paris in 1798—an accumulation of wealth, cultivation, profligacy, ferocity, and desperate ungodliness. The Cainite race represented, with a certain terrific loyalty, the seed of the serpent."—*Humphrey.* This closes the history of Cain and his descendants. "The curtain falls on the race of Cain with this picture of savage ferocity, glorying in revenge and merciless in its fury. What nations sprang from this earliest separation of the human family is not told us; for there is no hint, even, in the names of Cain's descendants that have survived."—*Geikie, p.* 146.

FIRST PERIOD. 31

SECTION 5. THE SETHITES.

GEN. 4:25-26; 5:1-32.

OUTLINE.

I. Seth.
Humphrey's Sacred Hist., etc., pp. 91-92.
Geikie's Hours, p. 146.
Butler's Bible Work, Gen.
Bible Dict., "Seth."

II. The Sethite Line.
Same references.

III. The Sethite and Cainite Lines Compared.
Same references.

IV. The Genealogies.
Humphrey, p. 108.
Geikie's Hours, p. 147.

NOTES.

I. Seth. Gen. 4:25 ; 5:3.
1. *Meaning of his Name.* 4:25. "The giving of this name indicated in Eve a good hope, if not an abiding faith in the promise of a holy seed, and a belief that this seed, destroyed in the death of Abel, was to be renewed in Seth."
2. *His Character.* Although born in the likeness of fallen Adam (5:3), the inference is that he was like godly Abel in character. 4:26.
3. *Father of a Godly Race.* 4:26. "Then began men to call on the name of the LORD." This the first notice of *public* worship. This brief clause indicates : (1) A general reformation, as

it would seem; (2) the introduction of public and social worship; (3) the name Jehovah significant. This God's covenant name, applied to him as Saviour.

II. The Sethite Line.

1. *This Line Traced Through Ten Generations in Fifth Chapter of Genesis—from Adam to Noah.*
2. *The Narrative for the Most Part a Bare Record of Births and Deaths.* "There is something very impressive in this antediluvian record of deaths; the long periods of life only make it more so. It tells forcibly of there being no escape from this law. The cadence of 'and he died' recurs with the effect of a tolling bell upon the imagination, and the length of interval between them adds to the solemnity of the lesson so given forth."
3. *Notable Names in this Line.*
    (1) Enoch. Concerning him two things deserve special notice: (*a*) He was a prophet. Read his prophecy in Jude 14–15. (*b*) He was translated. 5:24; cf. *Heb.* 11:5.
    (2) Noah. 5:28–29.
4. *The Most Important Thing Concerning the Sethite Line is yet to be Mentioned—it was the Messianic Line. Luke* 3:37–38.

III. The Sethite and Cainite Lines Compared.

Note (1) the similarity of the names in the two lists (2) the contrast in the meaning of the names in the two lists—a favorable meaning in the line of Seth, an unfavorable meaning in that of Cain (*Geikie*).

IV. The Genealogies.

Importance. 1. "They establish the fact that all mankind descended from one man and one woman. This truth is fundamental to revealed religion, because it points out the indissoluble connection between the lost estate of all mankind and the disobedience of their common progenitor; and it lays the foundation for a plan of redemption that shall be one plan and yet applicable to every member of the race."

2. "The registers call our attention also to the longevity of the patriarchs. The proof by which the longevity is established, the vital forces to which it is to be referred, and its results, historical and moral, should be considered."

3. "The historical uses of this longevity are conspicuous. In the absence of the art of writing, it secured the transmission, through the memory of the long-lived people, of useful inventions and discoveries, together with such knowledge as might be gathered by observation and study. It afforded the means, also, for the preservation of primeval history. . . Methuselah was contemporary with Adam two hundred and fifty years and with Shem one hundred; Shem was contemporary with Abraham one hundred years and with Isaac fifty."—*Humphrey.*

SECTION 6. THE FLOOD.

GEN. 6; 7; 8:1-19.

OUTLINE.

I. The Cause of the Flood. The Second Apostasy.
Humphrey's Sacred Hist., chap. 7.
Price's Syllabus, p. 34.
Geikie's Hours, chap. 13.
Butler's Bible Work, Gen.

II. The Ark.
Dods on Gen.
Humphrey's Sacred Hist., chap. 8.
Other references same as above.

III. The Flood Prevails.
References same as above.

NOTES.

I. The Cause of the Flood—the Second Apostasy.

The first apostasy was that of Adam and Eve in Eden. The second apostasy was that of the race which reached its culmination just prior to the flood. Concerning this apostasy notice:

1. *It Seems to have been Gradual.* There is reason to believe that in the time of Seth and Enoch the state of religion in the family of Seth was gratifying and hopeful. Gen. 4:26. But in the time of Enoch the apostasy had made great progress. Jude 14–15.

2. *The Culmination of the Apostasy.* Gen. 6:5–6. See also vs. 11–12.

3. *The Primary Cause of this Apostasy, the Depravity of Human Nature.* 6:5; cf. Matt. 15:19–20.
4. *The Circumstances which Developed and Hastened the Apostasy.* 6:1–2. "Nothing could be more preposterous than the vagary of the intermarriage of angels with the daughters of men. . . . The obvious sense of the text corresponds with the plan of the narrative. The statement that 'the sons of God' (the Sethites) 'saw the daughters of men' (the Cainites) corresponds to what is said before of the sensuous charms of the wives and daughters of Lamech. The words 'they took them wives of all which they chose' indicates, it may be, not only the mixed marriages, but the introduction among the Sethites of the Cainite usage of polygamy."— *Humphrey.*
5. *The Sentence.* v. 7. This sentence, however, was not to be executed at once. v. 3. Why not?
6. *The Exception to the General Sentence.* v. 8. *Noah.*—(*a*) His character. vs. 8–9. (*b*) His family. v. 10. (*c*) God's command to Noah. vs. 13–22. (*d*) Noah's occupation besides building the ark. 1 Pet. 3:18–20. Who went and preached? Christ. By what agency? His Spirit. Through what instrumentality? Noah. 2 Pet. 2:5. To whom did he preach? "The contemporaries of Noah, the disobedient who perished by the flood after God had suffered long with them." When was this preaching done? In the time during which God was waiting in patience on the disobedient, through an hundred and twenty years, while the ark was in building. What and where were those people

when Peter wrote his epistle? They were lost spirits shut up in perdition.

II. The Ark.

1. *Instructions for Building the Ark.* Gen. 6:13-16. It was to be an *ark;* not a ship (because not sailing power but only abundant storage and steadiness in the water were required), but a floating house or box, made of gopher (probably cypress) wood and rendered thoroughly water-tight by being covered with bitumen within and without. It was to be divided into compartments (rooms, lit. nests) for the more convenient distribution of the various animals; and these rooms were to be in three tiers, one above the other, in lower, second, and third stories. The entire structure was to be 300 cubits long, 50 broad, and 30 high; or taking the cubit as equal to 21 inches—525 feet long, 87 feet 6 inches broad, and 52 feet 6 inches high. The *Great Eastern* was 680 feet long, 83 broad, and 58 high. Ten buildings the size of Solomon's temple could have been stored away in the ark. The proportions have been tested. Peter Jansen, a Dutchman, had a ship built of the same proportions, though on a smaller scale, and found it well adapted to freightage."—*Dods on Gen.*

2. *The Purpose of the Ark.* vs. 17–22. For preserving, (*a*) Noah and his family, v. 18, and (*b*) two "of every living thing," vs. 19–20.

3. *The Entrance into the Ark.* 7:1–16. (1) Time of entrance. (2) Contents. (3) "As the Lord commanded Noah."

III. The Flood Prevails.

7:11–12 and 17–24.

1. *The Execution of the Sentence Previously Pronounced.* Cf. 6 : 7, 13, 17, with 7 : 19–23.

2. *The Extent of the Flood.* Two views: (1) That it was universal. (2) That it was limited. The arguments in favor of each of these views are admirably summarized in Price's Syllabus of Old Testament History, p. 35, as follows : " I. *For* its universality: *a*, the language of chap. 6 : 17 ; 6 : 4, 19, 21, 23 ; *but* (1) earth was used (a) of Palestine alone. Joel 1 : 2 ; Ps. 44 : 3 ; (b) of a field ; Ex. 23 : 10 ; (2) limitations (a) in Acts 2:5: " Every nation under heaven; (b) cf. Rom.1:8, throughout the whole (known) world ; (c) cf. Matt. 12 : 42 : " The queen of the South came from the ends of the earth ; *b*, the common tradition among all peoples ; *but*, this only strengthens the view that all people are the offspring of one pair. II. *Against* its universality: *a*, Scientific difficulties : (1) Amount of water required would disarrange the solar system ; (2) vegetation would perish in such continued submergence ; (3) fish would not survive in foreign waters ; *b*, practical difficulties : (1) collecting of such animals as the sloth, polar bear and kangaroo ; (2) preservation of 120,000 kinds of insects ; (3) preservation of 100,000 species of plants ; *c*, physical evidences : (1) Undisturbed volcanic remains at Auvergne, France ; (2) certified age of trees in Mexico and Senegal ; *d*, probable similar geologic movements in the past ; *e*, the real purpose of the deluge."

3. *The Duration of the Flood.* Gen. 7:17; 8:14. "The rain began on the 17th day of the second month, or about the beginning of November, and Noah left the ark on the 27th of the same month in the following year."—*Dods on Gen.*

4. *The Place where the Ark Rested.* 8:4. Not, of course, on the peak (Masis), which is 17,000 feet high and covered with perpetual snow, and on which, consequently, many of the animals must have perished with cold, while even the hardiest must have been killed in the descent, which is practicable only to skilled mountaineers. It seems probable that Ararat was the name descriptive of the lofty Armenian table-land which overlooks the plain of the Araxes on the north, and of Mesopotamia on the south."—*Dods.*

SECTION 7. THE SECOND BEGINNING.
Gen. 8:15; 9:1-29.

OUTLINE.

I. Noah's Sacrifice.
Humphrey's Sacred Hist., chap. 9.
Price's Syllabus, p. 37.
Commentaries.

II. Divine Revelations made to Noah.
Same references.

III. Noah's After-History.
Same references.

NOTES.

The Flood marked a great epoch in the world's history. The entire human race had been destroyed with the exception of the eight souls in the Ark. As they descend from the Ark, at the command of God, the race is to make a new beginning under new conditions and circumstances. Very aptly, therefore, does Dr. Price call this epoch "The Second Beginning," both like and unlike the first beginning in Eden. Noah's first act was to build an altar unto the Lord. This is the first altar mentioned in the Bible. From this time "the altar became the central object in the life of the patriarchs, and in the Hebrew ritual; it was the genesis also of the future tabernacle and temple." Upon this altar Noah offered sacrifice.

I. Noah's Sacrifice. 8:20.

FEATURES—

1. *Its Extent.* v. 20.
2. *Bloody Sacrifice—Atonement.*
3. *Burnt Offering.* This the first occurrence of the burnt offering in Scripture, and the original of Lev. 1:3. Meaning of burnt offering? "The sum of the matter is, that Noah's oblation was expiatory and prophetical; it involved confession of guilt, the remission of sin by shedding of blood, and it pointed forward to the way of salvation, by the sacrifice of Christ." God accepted Noah's offering, v. 21; and upon the ground of his sacrifice God deliberately determines ("The Lord said in his heart") to make certain most important revelations to Noah.

II. Divine Revelations to Noah.

1. *A Promise.* 8:21–22. This, a very great temporal promise, giving assurance of the stability and regularity of Nature; given not on the ground of man's righteousness (v. 21), but on the ground of the sacrifice.

2. *The Blessing.* 9:1. God here gives to Noah and his sons the possession of the earth. The terms in which the original grant was made to Adam were repeated to Noah. The grant to both was introduced with a blessing. Cf. Gen. 1:29.

3. Gen. 9:2. *God Gave to Them also a Qualified Dominion over the Lower Animals.* Cf. Gen. 1:28. "In Adam it was a dominion of absolute authority; in Noah a lordship of fear and dread. . . . We recognize here indelible signs both of the gift of the earth and the curse upon it for man's sake."

4. *Animal Food Given to Man.* "We are not at liberty to say that, in point of fact, flesh was not eaten by the antediluvians. We are told only that a divine permission to use it was now for the first time granted." This grant had, however, an important and strict limitation. v. 4. Reason, Lev. 17:10–11.

5. *Capital Punishment Enjoined.* vs. 5–6. This a passage of great importance. Notice:
   (1) The penalty of death is affixed to the crime of murder.
   (2) The reason of the law is here given: "For in the image of God made he man." "He who strikes at the life of a man strikes at God's image, and through his image at God himself."

(3) The brute beast killing a man must be slain.
(4) The minister charged with the infliction of the penalty is appointed. "At the hand of every man's brother will I require the life of man." "The Hebrew for 'every man's brother' signifies literally 'the one and the other,' meaning that God requires of every living man the blood of the murderer; there shall be no escape for the guilty, and no excuse for 'the other' who connives at his escape."
(5) The law is of universal and perpetual obligation. The law a divine command.
(6) "These two brief verses are by the soundest publicists held to contain the fundamental principles of civil government in the hands of a magistracy. The duty of protecting human life is enjoined on mankind."—*Humphrey.*
Behold in all this the sacredness of human life.

6. *The Covenant.* Sometimes called the Covenant of Forbearance.

Aspects of this Covenant:
(1) "The preservation of the earth from the waters of another flood is the sole promise conveyed by its terms, strictly interpreted."
(2) The promise in the covenant includes the lower animals. v. 10.
(3) The covenant was made with Noah and his sons, for themselves and their posterity. vs. 8-9. See here an example of the principle of representation.
(4) The idea of reciprocity wanting in this covenant.
(5) The seal of the covenant—the rainbow. A familiar object, which had existed from the

beginning, now became the sign of a new idea —the idea of a divine covenant. This bow a simple token of a covenant, not a sacrament.

III. Noah's After-History.

1. *Noah's Sin.* v. 21. "Attempts have been made to excuse Noah's conduct. But the plain, blunt words of Calvin are better than any apology: 'I rather suppose that we are to learn from the drunkenness of Noah what a filthy and detestable crime drunkenness is.'" Very closely connected with Noah's sin was the indecency of Ham: "It proceeded from a native-born spirit of indecency and of ribaldry and mockery toward all that is good. Ham's crime divided the sons of Noah into two parties, Ham and his posterity representing the seed of the serpent; Shem and Japheth, with their posterity, the seed of the woman."

2. *Noah's Prophecies Concerning His Sons.*
    (1) Canaan (Ham's son). v. 25. Also he was to be a servant to both his brethren. How fulfilled?
    (2) Shem (v. 26). "Noah's prophecy in regard to Shem took the form, not of a benediction on Shem, but of a doxology to God. . . The boon promised here is indicated by the name Jehovah God given to the Almighty. He is called, not Elohim, the general term describing the Divine Being, but by his greater name Jehovah, the God of redemption, the covenant-giving and covenant-keeping God, even he who had just entered into a special covenant with Noah. Next Jehovah is called the God of Shem. Never before, in Scripture, is the Almighty called the

God of any one person or race. But after this the distinguished honor follows the line of Shem throughout the ages. Jehovah is spoken of as the God of Abraham," etc. . . . . . This prophecy "foreshows the future exaltation of Shem over his brothers in his descendant Eber, and later still in the illustrious family of Abraham, with whom the far-famed covenant of circumcision was established. This prediction has been received by the Church as the second Messianic promise."

(3) Japheth. (v. 27.) Two elements in this prophecy—(1) worldly prosperity, (2) spiritual privileges. "Nothing in the history and present state of the world is better known than the fulfillment of this prophecy. God has enlarged Japheth. From the very beginning his sons became the emigrating, colonizing race, until they have passed by land and sea around the world. . . . . Not less certain is it that the posterity of Japheth have found the salvation which was bestowed on Shem. 'They dwell in the tents of Shem.'"—*Humphrey.*

SECTION 8. THE TABLE OF NATIONS.
Gen. 10.

OUTLINE.

I. The Value of this Table.
Humphrey, Sacred Hist., chap. 10.
Butler's Bible Work, Gen.

II. The Plan of the Table.
Humphrey, as above.
Dods, Genesis.
Price, Syllabus of O. T. Hist.

III. The Geography of the Table.
Humphrey, as above.
Price, as above.
Hurlbut, Manual of Bib. Geog., p. 23.

IV. The Sons of Japheth.
Humphrey, etc.
Price, etc.
Hurlbut, etc.
Blaikie, Bible Hist., chap. 3.
Butler's Bible Work.
Geikie, Hours.
Dods, Genesis.

V. The Sons of Ham.
Same references.

VI. The Sons of Shem.
Same references.

VII. The Accuracy of the Table.
Same references.

NOTES.

I. The Value of this Table.
1. *As a Proof of the Unity of the Race.* "The descent of all mankind from Noah is, of course, a renewed testimony by scripture to the unity of the human race—a doctrine so intimately connected with the divine plan of redemption, and so vital to the brotherhood and mutual sympathy of man with man."—*Geikie.*

2. *The Most Valuable Ethnological Chart in Existence.* "This document of less than fifty lines exhausts the science of the origin of nations; no other races have ever existed."

3. *Affords "Proof of the Prophetic Inspiration of Noah and Casts Light on the Plan of History Adopted by Moses."*

II. **The Plan of the Table.**

1. *Rests Historically on the Basis of the Flood.* "The compiler is careful to say that sons were born to Shem, Ham, and Japheth 'after the flood' (v. 1), and that, by the people descending from these, were the nations divided in the earth after the flood." v. 32.

2. *The Order in which the Sons of Noah are Mentioned in the Table.* The order is: Japheth, Ham, Shem. "But why did Moses give the first place to Japheth and the last to Shem? The answer is, that he first disposed of the races that branched off from the main line, and thus cleared the way for an uninterrupted history of the promised seed."

3. *The Evident Design of the Chapter is to Give the Origin of Nations rather than the History of Individuals.*

4. *The Intimate Connection between the Messianic Prophecies of Noah and these Genealogies.* Salvation, said Noah, shall come to the race through the family of Shem. Accordingly, the register gives all the links between Shem and Abraham. Japheth was to find salvation in the tents of Shem. So his pedigree is preserved. Nor is Ham left out of the list.

III. The Geography of the Table.

"Let two lines be drawn on the map from west to east; the one from the southern, the other from the northern border of Palestine. The territory between these two parallels was the portion of Shem. Ham took his inheritance below Shem's southern line. Japheth made his home north of Shem's upper line." This suggestion only true in a general sense. "Noah foretold the destiny which awaited the posterity of his three sons. . . . But these destinies were all bound up with their future homes on the surface of the earth. Let it be imagined that Japheth and Ham had missed their ways, Japheth going to the torrid zone and Ham to the northern temperate latitudes; and then let us imagine the confusion which this misplacement would have introduced into Noah's scheme of prophecy."—*Humphrey.*

IV. The Sons of Japheth. vs. 2-5.

Mention the principal nations which descended from Japheth.

V. The Sons of Ham. vs. 6-20.

Principal Hamitic nations.

VI. The Sons of Shem. vs. 21-31.

Principal Semitic nations.

VII. The Accuracy of the Table.

"The Jews maintain, as an article of faith, that the whole of the tenth chapter of Genesis is as fully and directly inspired as are the words, 'I am the Lord your God.' The Christian need not hesitate to subscribe that article. It does not profess to embrace all the peoples in existence at this time; but it is complete and sufficient to the end for which it was compiled ; it is a commentary on Noah's Messianic prophecy, and a preface to the history of Abraham. Its omissions are as essential to its proper uses as its contents. More than that, every word of it is true. No contradictions between its details and the findings of sound ethnological science has been discovered. It is entitled to carry on its face, not the *caveat*, ' errors excepted.' but the challenge, ' errors nowhere.' "—*Humphrey.*

SECTION 9. BABEL.
Gen. 11.

OUTLINE.

I. **The Relation of this Chapter to the Preceding.**
Humphrey's Sacred Hist., chap. 11.
Butler's Bible Work, Gen.

II. **The Tower.**
Humphrey's Sacred Hist.
Blaikie, Manual, p. 44.
Price, Syllabus Old Testament Hist., p. 39.
Butler's Bible Work, Genesis.
Bible Dict.

III. **The Purposes of the Tower.**
Same references.

IV. **The Confusion of Tongues.**
Same references.

V. **Pentecost and Babel.**
Humphrey's Sacred Hist.

NOTES.

I. The Relation of this Chapter to the Preceding.
The tenth chapter gives an account of the dispersion of mankind; the eleventh gives the cause of the dispersion. It follows, therefore, that in order of time the events recorded in the eleventh chapter preceded the events recorded in the tenth.

II. The Tower. vs. 1-4.
1. *Location.* The land of Shinar, on the Mesopotamian plain. "Several of the most eminent Orientalists believe that the ruins known as Borsippa or Birs Nimrod represent it."—*Dods.* These ruins are near the site of Babylon.
2. *Material.* v. 3.
3. *The Builders.* It seems from the record in Genesis that the whole race were united in this enterprise.

III. The Purposes of the Tower.
1. *To Make Themselves Famous.* v. 4.
2. *To Prevent Their Dispersion.* v. 4; but 9:1-7.
3. *Probably for Idolatrous Purposes.* "In its essence, therefore, the building of the tower was a Titanic ungodly enterprise."

IV. The Confusion of Tongues.
1. *The Unity of Language when They Began to Build the Tower.* v. 1. "More literally, 'of one lip and word.' By the lip is meant the tongue or pronunciation, including the vocal inflections; by the 'word' is meant the vocabulary. All the living had one word for each idea, and one way of pronouncing that word. They were one in speech, just as they were one in origin from Noah."

2. *Their Language Confounded.* v. 7. "We have no information as to the way in which this was effected." Probably the original unity of speech was now broken up into three languages. Gen. 10:5, 20, 31.
3. *This Confusion of Language Due to Direct Divine Interposition.* 5–9. "The narrative takes the form of a vivid anthropo-morphism."
4. *The Dispersion.* vs. 8–9. This the result of the confusion of language.

V. Babel and Pentecost.

"Biblical scholars concur in accepting the miracle of the Pentecost as the antithesis and reversal of the miracle at Babel. In the words of Grotius: 'The punishment of tongues dispersed mankind; the gift of tongues gathered the dispersed into one people.' Babel represents God's judgment on the impiety of man driving them asunder; Pentecost represents the work of the Holy Spirit, restoring man by the righteousness of faith to unity again."—*Humphrey.*

REVIEW CHART OF THE FIRST PERIOD.

OUTLINE OF PERIOD.

SEC. 1. Creation.

    First Day—Light.
    Second Day—Firmament.
    Third Day—Seas and Dry Land; Vegetable Kingdom.
    Fourth Day—Sun, Moon, Stars.
    Fifth Day—Oviparous Animals.
    Sixth Day—Higher Land Animals; Man.
    Seventh Day—Sabbath.
    Creation as a whole.

SEC. 2. Man.

    I. The Peculiarities of Man's Creation.
    II. Eden.
    III. Woman.
    IV. The Covenant of Works.
    V. The Four Primeval Ordinances.

SEC. 3. The Fall.

    I. The Test of Man's Obedience.
    II. The Temptation.
    III. The Sin whereby Adam Fell.
    IV. The Fall.
    V. The Guilty Pair before the Great Judge.

SEC. 5. The Sethites.

    I. Seth.
    II. The Sethite Line.
    III. Sethite and Cainite Line Compared.
    IV. The Genealogies.

SEC. 6. The Flood.

    I. The Cause of the Flood.
    II. The Ark.
    III. The Flood Prevails.

SEC. 7. The Second Beginning.

    I. Noah's Sacrifice.
    II. Divine Revelations to Noah.
    III. Noah's After-History.

SEC. 8. The Table of Nations.

    I. The Value of this Table.
    II. The Plan of the Table.
    III. The Geography of the Table.
    IV. The Sons of Japheth.
    V. The Sons of Ham.
    VI. The Sons of Shem.
    VII. The Accuracy of the Table.

I. Early History of Cain and Abel.
II. Cain's Great Crime.
III. Cain before the Divine Judge.
IV. Cain in the Land of Nod.

II. The Tower.
III. The Purposes of the Tower.
IV. The Confusion of Tongues.
V. Pentecost and Babel.

QUESTIONS ON THE PERIOD.

1. Why is this Period called Ante-Ecclesiastical?
2. What does the work of creation teach concerning God?
3. Why is the narrative of creation placed first in the Bible?
4. What is the importance of the narrative of Man's creation and primeval state.
5. What are the principal features of the First Messianic Promise.
6. What are the most important points in the history of the Cainite line?
7. What is the teaching of the Narrative of Deluge on the subject of God, of Sin, and of Salvation?
8. What were the most important features of the revelations made to Noah?
9. What the historical and religious value of the Table of Nations?
10. What the most important points in the history of Babel.
11. Name in order the principal events, persons, and places in the history of the period.

TOPICS FOR SPECIAL STUDY.

1. Different theories of the origin of the universe.
2. The Mosaic Narrative of Creation.
3. The Superiority of the Bible stories of Creation, the Fall, Cain and Abel, Flood, and Babel.
4. The Names of the Deity in the Period.
5. The Covenants of the Period.
6. Salvation in the Period.
7. God in the History of the Period.

SECOND PERIOD.

POST-ECCLESIASTICAL.

FROM THE CALL OF ABRAM TO EXODUS—432 YEARS.
GEN. 11 : 27 to 25 : 11.

SECTION 1. ABRAHAM.

OUTLINE.

Introduction.
Humphrey, Sacred Hist., Chaps. 12, 13.
Blaikie, Manual, Chap. 4.
Butler's Bible Work—Gen.
Price, Syllabus O. T. Hist.

I. Before the Giving of the Covenant.
Same references.

II. The Covenant.
Same references.

III. After the Giving of the Covenant.
Same references.

IV. The Prominence of Abraham in Bible.
Same references.

NOTES.

Introduction.

1. *Condition of the World at the Call of Abram.* "True religion almost extinct. Among the three groups of nations descending from Shem, Ham and Japheth, the divine revelations to Adam and Noah were forgotten or disfigured. Idolatry, a sin unknown to the generations before the deluge, but conceived at Babel, was steadily gaining ground. Both the true and the false worship were, in the well chosen words of Hengstenberg, 'in a transition state, idolatry on the increase, true religon on the wane.'"

2. *The Call of Abram Marks a New Era in the Kingdom of God.* Hitherto "the divine revelations were not restricted to a single individual or family. The first promise was made to the seed of the woman in general. . . . Access to God at the altar was granted to every holy worshipper. . . . There was on earth no favored people in the bosom of which the kingdom of heaven was established." The administration of redemption was catholic or œcumenical. Now, however, a great change takes place. "The Almighty chose out of the human race one man, a native of Mesopotamia, called Abram, changed his name to Abraham, the father of many nations, separated him and his household from his native country and kindred, made an everlasting covenant with him and his seed after him, and established in that single household his church and kingdom on earth."—*Humphrey.*

3. *"The Call of Abram may be Treated as the Opening of the Theophanic Era,* an era which culminated with the incarnation and life on earth of the Son of God." " The term 'theophany' is derived from the Greek and is applied to the appearance of the God of glory to the senses of man." Ten theophanies were granted to Abram, viz.:

(1) In Mesopotamia. Acts 7:2; Gen. 12:1.
(2) Shechem. Gen. 12:7.
(3) Bethel. Gen. 13:14.
(4) Mamre. Gen. 15:1.
(5) " " 17:1.
(6) " " 18:1.
(7) " " 21:12.
(8) " " 22:1.
(9) Mount Moriah. Gen. 22:11.
(10) " " Gen. 22:15.

4. *The Genealogy of Abram.* Gen. 11:10–26. Thus Abram is connected with Shem, Noah, Seth, and Adam.

I. Abram before the Giving of the Covenant.

1. *The Call.*
   (1) The manner in which the call was given. Acts 7:2. This the first theophany to Abram. "The God of glory"—"appeared"—"unto our father Abraham"—"when he was in Mesopotamia before he dwelt in Haran." (Study each clause.)
   (2) This call embraced: (*a*) A twofold command, expatriation, and segregation. Acts 7:3; Gen. 12:1. (*b*) A series of promises. Gen. 12:1–3. (These promises afterward embodied in the covenant, which see.)

2. *From Ur of the Chaldees to his Going Down to Egypt.* During this period three important events are recorded: (1) The departure from Ur in obedience to the call of God and the sojourn at Haran. 11:31, 32. (2) The entrance into Canaan. 12:4–9. At Shechem he had his second theophany, in which God promised to his seed the land of Canaan. v. 7. Here also, he built an altar (v. 7), as he did also at Bethel. v. 8. (3) The famine which led him to go to Egypt. v. 10.

3. *His Sojourn in Egypt.* While here occurred his disgraceful fall, which led to his expulsion from the land. vs. 11–20.

4. *From his Return to Canaan to the Giving of the Covenant.* The principal events of this period:

(1) The separation from Lot. 13:5–13 (exp.).

(2) Abram's third theophany. vs. 14–17. Notice the promises embraced in this theophany. How timely!

(3) Abram makes his abode at Mamre. v. 18. Observe the frequent recurrence of the altar. Abram has been called the man of the tent and the altar.

(4) The rescue of Lot. 14:1–17 and 21–24.

(5) Melchizedek. vs. 18–20; cf. Hebrews 7: 1–11. "Melchizedek was a Canaanite, a holy man, a king of righteousness and a priest of the Most High God, holding a priesthood of an exceptional order among the heathen. He blessed Abram in God's behalf: 'Blessed be Abram of the Most High God, possessor of heaven and earth,' and again he thanked God on Abram's behalf: 'And blessed be the Most

SECOND PERIOD. 55

High God which hath delivered thine enemies into thy hand.' His act was an authoritative assurance to Abram that God had called him to take up arms and had given him the victory. This is the only military expedition undertaken by the pilgrim father. We should miss its historical significance if we should recognize nothing in it except, first, an indication of Abram's courage and strategy as a fighting man; and, next, an impulse of affection for his undeserving kinsman. It illustrates the faith of Abram; 'he fights once as he walks always, by faith.' Moreover, the divine help which was granted to him in the campaign and the blessing of God pronounced upon him by the royal priest, prove that he was, by the grace of God, the lawful heir, the lord paramount of the land of promise, and that he held a divine commission to protect, by force of arms, the sacred soil on which the plan of salvation for the world was to be matured."—*Humphrey.*

(6) The fourth theophany. Gen. 15: 1. The occasion which called forth this theophany, and the wonderful interview connected with it, was the despondency of Abram after the return from the "slaughter of the kings." This despondency seems to have been due chiefly to two things: (*a*) The fact that he had no legitimate heir. vs. 2–3. (*b*) The fact that hostilities might be renewed by the kings of the East, and the land taken from him. Thus the divine promises of a seed and of the land would be defeated. It seems to have been the object of the Lord in this chapter to comfort

and reassure Abram on these two points—the *seed* and the *land*. Concerning the *seed*, the chapter contains two important revelations: First, the assurance of a legitimate heir and a numerous posterity (vs. 4–5); second, prophecies as to his posterity and as to his own peaceful end (vs. 13–16). Concerning the *land*, the chapter also contains two revelations: First, the promise of the land is renewed (v. 7); second, the boundaries defined. These promises and revelations concerning the *seed* and the *land* are confirmed by a covenant. vs. 8–12, 18. This transaction recorded in the fifteenth chapter may be regarded as the first stage of the Abrahamic Covenant.

(7) The story of Hagar. Gen. 16. The chapter falls into two divisions: (*a*) The scheme of Sarah to help God fulfill his promise concerning the seed (vs. 1–4); in this scheme all parties appear in a bad light: (*b*) the results of the scheme—discord in the home, sorrow, failure (vs. 5–16). "In this unpretending, domestic chapter, we have laid bare to us the origin of one of the most striking facts in the history of religion, viz.: that from the one person of Abram have sprung Christianity, and that religion which has been, and still is, its most formidable rival, Mohammedanism. To Ishmael, Abram's first-born, all the Arab tribes are proud to trace their pedigree, and in Mohammed they see the fulfillment of the promise given to the great patriarch."—*Dods*.

With the sixteenth chapter ends the first division of the history of Abram.

II. The Abrahamic Covenant—Introductory.

1. *The Fourth of the Series of Covenants Recorded in the Scriptures.* (1) The Covenant of Works. (2) The Covenant of Grace. (3) The Covenant of Forbearance. (4) The Covenant of Circumcision, or the Abrahamic Covenant.

2. *The Importance of this Covenant.* (1) The provisions of this Covenant are integral elements in the plan of redemption. (2) These provisions controlled the career of the nations and kings who descended from Abraham. (3) The charter of the visible church.

3. *The Position of the Covenant in the History of Abraham.* According to Dr. Humphreys (p. 229), the covenant was begun in the fourth theophany (Gen. 15) was enlarged in the fifth (Gen. 17), and completed in the tenth (Gen. 22). Dr. H. adds: "Now the significant fact is that the promises which were put into the formal covenant and made part thereof, are nearly identical with the promises contained in the seven other theophanic revelations." Hence the covenant is the great central feature, the climax of the history of Abraham.

THE COVENANT.

1. The Parties—God and Abram. 15:18; 17:2.
2. The Subject—Salvation. 17:7.
3. God's Part—Series of Promises.
4. Abram's Part—Faith and Obedience.
5. Sanctions—Adoption and Excision.
6. The Seal—Circumcision.

EXPOSITION OF THE COVENANT.

1. *The Parties*—
    (1) God, the Almighty, "A Spirit infinite, eternal, and unchangeable in his being, wisdom, power, holiness, justice, goodness, and truth." For *this* God to enter into covenant with man was an act of infinite condescension and grace. (2) Abram. In this transaction Abram is to be considered in two aspects: (*a*) As an individual. It had been thirty-nine years since God had called him in Ur, and twenty-four years since he came out of Haran. These were doubtless years of training, during which God was fitting him for the position he was to hold in the covenant transaction. (*b*) As a representative. The covenant was made with Abram for himself and his posterity. Gen. 17:7.

2. *The Subject—Salvation.* That this is the subject seems evident from Gen. 17:7. In what other sense was he to be a God unto Abraham than a Saviour? Was not this the most important and supreme sense in which he was to be his God and the God of his posterity? Cf. Rom. 4:16, and Gal. 3:7–9 and 13–14.

3. *God's Part a Series of Promises.*
    (1) An immense posterity. 17:4–6. This promise previously given is here repeated, and in token of its certain fulfillment and importance his name changed from Abram to *Abraham.* This promise could not be *perfectly* fulfilled in Israel according to the flesh. But see Rom. 4:16–17. Hence, included not only his posterity according to the flesh,

but also his spiritual seed. Gal. 3 : 29. Has this promise been yet fulfilled? Gen. 17 : 5.

(2) The land of Canaan for himself and his posterity. Gen. 17 : 8. In the first stage of the covenant the boundaries of this land were defined. Gen. 15 : 18-21. In the second stage of the covenant the gift was secured to Abraham for an everlasting possession. But did the literal land of Canaan *exhaust* this promise? Is it capable of accommodating *all* his posterity? Did Abraham himself understand that nothing but the literal land of Canaan was intended? See Heb. 11 : 9, 10, 13-16. Has this promise of the covenant been fulfilled in its most important sense?

(3) The divine blessing on him and on them. 17 : 7. The same blessing promised to both.

(4) Salvation to be conveyed through him to all the world. Gen. 22 : 18. Who is this "seed"? See Gal. 3 : 16. This the third Messianic promise and the consummate promise of the covenant. Has this promise been fulfilled?

4. *The Sanctions of the Covenant.* By sanction is meant to render sacred or inviolable, to fix unalterably.

(1) Adoption. By adoption is meant the blessed relation which Abraham and his seed, according to this covenant, are henceforth to sustain to God.

(2) Excision. By this is meant the exclusion of the offspring of Abraham, near and remote, from the rights and privileges of the covenant. Excision was both sovereign and penal.

Sovereign in the case of Ishmael and Esau; penal to the disobedient. 17:14.
5. *The Seal of the Covenant.* vs. 10-11.
  (1) This a sacrament, the first and for 400 years the only sacrament of the visible church. What is a sacrament? "A sacrament is a holy ordinance instituted by Christ, wherein by sensible signs Christ and the benefits of the new covenant are represented, sealed, and applied to believers."
  (2) This sacrament the initiatory rite of the visible church. By this sacrament the people of God were separated from the world by an outward mark and sign. Hitherto the church has existed as invisible; henceforth it became an organized, visible body, separated from the world.
  (3) What did this rite signify? Two things: (*a*) Native depravity. Lev. 26:41; Acts 7:51. Hence uncircumcision in the Scriptures is a symbol of moral defilement. (*b*) The necessity of spiritual renovation. Deut. 30:6; Rom. 2:28-29. Note, however, that it only signified, did not effect, regeneration.
  (4) To whom was this rite to be applied? (*a*) To Abraham and the adult members of his household. (*b*) To the infant children of believers. 17:12.
  (5) This rite sealed to each of its subjects his personal interest in the covenant.
III. **Abraham after the Giving of the Covenant.**
  1. *The Sixth Theophany and Accompanying Events.* Chapters 18 and 19.
    (1) The Lord and two angels the guests of Abraham. 18:1-8. What a picture of hospitality!

(2) The Lord announces the birth of a son to Abraham and Sarah. vs. 9–15.
(3) Foretells to Abraham the doom of Sodom. 16–21. Note in this disclosure two things: (*a*) The testimony of the Lord to Abraham (17–19); (*b*) the reason for the destruction of Sodom (20–21).
(4) Abraham's intercession for Sodom, 23–33. In these verses we see the power of intercessory prayer; what blessings the presence of the righteous in this world may secure to the wicked!
(5) The fulfillment of the divine threatening against Sodom. Chap. 19.
(6) The rescue of Lot and his two daughters, but his wife destroyed.
(7) Moab and Ammon.

2. *Abraham in Gerar.* Chap. 20. Abraham's second fall.
3. *Birth of Isaac and Expulsion of Hagar and Ishmael.* 21:1–21. The seventh theophany. v. 12.
4. *Treaty with Abimelech.* 21:22–23.
5. *The Sacrifice of Isaac.* 22:1–19. This chapter contains three theophanies—the eighth, ninth, and tenth of the series.
   (1) The eighth theophany. vs. 1 and 2. Thus did God "tempt" or prove Abraham—test him. The test twofold: (*a*) Of his faith in God's character; (*b*) of his faith in the fulfillment of the covenant. Did Abraham stand the test? vs. 3–10. Cf. Heb. 11:17–19.
   (2) The ninth theophany. vs. 11–14.
   (3) The tenth theophany. vs. 15–18. This the final ratification of the covenant. "The occa-

sion was made memorable by the oath of Jehovah, the first solemnity of the kind on record."—*Humphrey.*

6. *Death and Burial of Sarah.* Chap. 23. Concerning this chapter Geikie says: "Nothing could be more touching in its simplicity or more true to the age than the picture of his bearing under his new trial, and of the incident attending the burial of the dead. .... The cave thus bought four thousand years ago lies on the east edge of Hebron, where an ancient church, built over it, is now turned into a mosque, which the Turks guard sacredly against any intrusion. Even the Crown Prince of Germany and the Prince of Wales could gain entrance only to the upper story, where there is next to nothing to see."—*Hours,* 308, 309. The interest attaching to this cave?

7. *Abraham's Second Marriage.* Gen. 25 : 1–6.

8. *Death and Burial.* 25 : 7–11.

IV. The Prominence Given to Abraham in the Bible.

This prominence shown.

1. *By the Space Given to his Biography.* "The history of the world for the first two thousand years is condensed into eleven chapters of Genesis, but the personal history of Abraham fills fourteen chapters of the book, and all the following Scriptures are occupied by the unfolding of the divine purpose, the rudiments of which were revealed to the great patriarch."

2. *By the Frequent Recurrence of his Name.* "The name Adam occurs eleven times in both Testaments; the name of Noah twenty times; but

that of Abraham is mentioned in about one hundred and twenty places, these being distributed not unequally throughout the entire Scriptures."
3. *In the Titles of Honor Applied to Him.* "Ab is equivalent to Father, Abram to High Father, and Abraham to The Father of Many Nations." (Gen. 17:5.) He is called the friend of God by historian, prophet, and apostle. (2 Chr. 20:7; Isa. 41:8; Jas. 2:23.) "Paul styles him 'Our Father Abraham,' 'The Father of all them that believe,' and 'Faithful Abraham.' Christ describes 'Abraham's bosom' 'as the heavenly rest.'"
4. *By the Position in the Genealogies.* The tables of genealogy and chronology in the antecedent history terminate with his name; and the tables which follow in Moses, in the Chronicles, in the Gospels, take their departure from him, and from Adam, and make their way through the ages to David, and through David and his royal line to Christ."—*Humphrey.* Explain the *ground of* this prominence, and its *bearing* upon the revelations made to Abraham.

SECTION 2. ISAAC.

Gen. 21:1-21; 22:1-19; 24; 26; 27:27-29 and 39-40; 28:3-4.

OUTLINE.

I. **From his Birth to his Marriage — a Period of Forty Years.**
Humphrey, Sacred Hist., chap. 22.
Geikie, Hours, chap. 23.
Price, Syllabus Old Testament Hist., p. 43.

II. **From his Marriage to his Death—a Period of 140 Years.**
Same references.

NOTES.

I. **From his Birth to his Marriage--a Period of Forty Years.**
  1. *His Birth Prophesied.* The prophecy. 15:4; 17:19; 18:9-11. The fulfillment. 21:1-3.
  2. *Circumcised the Eighth Day.* Gen. 21:4.
  3. *Sole Heir of the Covenant.* 17:19-21.
  4. *Mocked by Ishmael.* 21:8-12.
  5. *Offered Up.* 22:1-19.
  6. *His Marriage.* Gen. 24.

II. **From his Marriage to his Death—a Period of 140 Years.**
Isaac's life after his marriage was uneventful. He was little more than a connecting link in the chain of the promised seed between Abraham his father, and Jacob his son. No new promise was made to him. No further development or explanation of the Abrahamic covenant distinguished his life.

1. Isaac in Gerar.
    (1) Famine in Canaan. 26:1.
    (2) First theophany. 26:2–5. God here renews the covenant made with Abraham.
    (3) Isaac's fall. vs. 7–10.
    (4) His prosperity. vs. 12–14.
2. Isaac in Beersheba. v. 23. His second theophany. v. 24.
3. The Covenant with Abimelech. vs. 26–31.
4. Prophecies Concerning his Sons. 27:27–29; 39, 40; 28:3–4.
5. His Old Age, Death, and Burial. 35:28–29.

SECTION 3. JACOB AND ESAU.
Gen. 25:19–34; 27:1–40.

OUTLINE.
(Introductory.)
I. The Difference between Jacob and Esau.
   Humphrey, Sacred Hist., chap. 23.
   Geikie, Hours, pp. 320–322.
II. The Sale of the Birthright.
   Same references.
III. Jacob Supplants Esau.
   Same references.

NOTES.
Introductory. The Twin Sons of Isaac and Rebecca.
   1. The Oracle at their Birth. Gen. 25:23; Mal. 1:2–3; Rom. 9:11–13.

2. *The Significance of the Minute Narrative.* The position of Jacob and Esau in the after-history.

I. The Difference between Jacob and Esau.

1. *In Personal Appearance.* Esau shaggy, hairy; Jacob smooth. Gen. 27:11.
2. *In Employment.* Esau "was a cunning hunter, a man of the field; abandoning the pastoral life of his race for the perils and stratagems of the chase, and for the wild and roving habits of the Bedouin. He has been called the after-play of Nimrod." "Jacob was a plain man, dwelling in tents." "He preferred the life of the shepherd to the life of the hunter, pitching his tents quietly in the midst of his flocks and herds.
3. *In Character.* Esau was a bold, reckless, sensual man caring more for self-indulgence than for spiritual things. He was, however, open, manly, and even at times magnanimous and forgiving. But his understanding was narrow, his appetite clamorous, and his disposition wayward; a natural born sensualist and profane person. Heb. 12:16.

" In Jacob, on the other hand, we see the best as well as the worst qualities of his race. If the earlier half of his life shows much that is unworthy, even through it there runs that thoughtful foresight and steadfast pursuit of a great aim which alone secures lasting and noble results."— *Geikie.*

II. The Sale of the Birthright. Gen. 25:29-34.

1. *Esau's Part in this Transaction.* The sale of his birthright for a mess of lentils. The birthright is thought to have embraced the following

benefits and blessings, during and after the patriarchal age :

(1) The office of Priesthood. Numb. 3:12-13.
(2) Supremacy in the family, the first-born succeeding to the dignity and authority of the father. 2 Chron. 21:3.
(3) Inheriting a double portion of the patrimony. Deut. 21:17.
(4) Moreover, Isaac's first-born was apparently, at least, the natural heir to the promises made to Abraham for his seed, including the land of Canaan, a great and powerful posterity, and the special favor of God.
(5) "He should also in his generation be the progenitor of Jesus Christ and the channel through which salvation should flow to the world." "The sin and folly attached to the sale of such a birthright 'for one morsel of meat' are not exaggerated in the Scriptures."

2. *Jacob's Part*. Jacob, in a crafty and cunning manner, took an ungenerous and dishonorable advantage of his brother. He knew he was not giving any adequate return for the birthright, and yet his eagerness to get it showed that he *valued* it.

III. Jacob Supplants Esau.

Gen. 27:1-29. An interval of forty-five years had elapsed, according to Dr. Humphrey (336), since the sale of the birthright. Isaac was now 137 and Jacob and Esau 74 years old. Read the chapter carefully and note (1) the condition of Isaac (1-2) and the part he took in the transaction; (2) Esau's part; (3) Rebecca's part; (4) Jacob's part. This a memorable, disgraceful, and painful scene at the bedside of an old man. What occurred here made an indelible impression upon all parties. This scene not only determined the after-history of Jacob and Esau, but indicates the national history which had its rise in these men. The main object of the historian was to explain how the purposes of God were accomplished in opposition to the perverse will of man, and to trace out the course of providence by which Jacob's position as the heir of the covenant was established. Let the following points in the narrative be considered:

1. *It appears that Isaac, being the head of the family, was the chief instrument in the accomplishment of the divine purpose.* Was he inspired in bestowing the blessings upon his sons? Heb. 11: 20.
2. *The Blessing Pronounced upon Jacob.* 27: 28–29. This secured to Jacob only the temporal benefits of the Abrahamic covenant. The other part of the blessing is in 28: 3–4. This fixes the position of Jacob as the heir of the promises to Abraham and as one of the Messianic line.
3. *The Blessing Pronounced upon Esau.* vs. 39, 40. "Isaac's legacy to Esau has been called 'a modified sentence.' It was a direct antithesis to Jacob's inheritance."
4. *Was Isaac right in trying to bestow the blessing of the covenant upon Esau?* Esau was the firstborn. Dr. Humphrey thinks that Isaac must have known that he was proposing to disregard the divine oracle at the birth of his sons; that Esau had by his alien marriages voluntarily forsaken the chosen seed and identified himself

SECOND PERIOD. 69

with the rejected races around him, and that he had despised his birthright.

5. *The means by which Rebecca and Jacob obtained the birthright or blessing were only evil.* They were not only sinful in themselves, but showed a lack of faith.

6. *For the sin of all the parties each one reaped a bitter harvest.* Isaac's home was blighted and broken; Rebecca was separated for life from her beloved Jacob; Jacob had to become an exile and was himself cheated and deceived by others; Esau became a freebooter, abandoning his home in Canaan for the desert of Edom.

7. *Notwithstanding all the sinful complications, God's purpose was carried out.* Ps. 76:10.

SECTION 4. JACOB.
GEN. 25: 21–34; CHAPS. 27 TO 49.

OUTLINE.

I. From his Birth to his Flight.
Humphrey, Sacred Hist., chap. 23.
Butler's Bible Work, Gen.
Geikie, Hours, chap. 23.

II. From his Flight to his Return to Canaan.
Humphrey, Sacred Hist., chap. 24.
Price, Syllabus, sec. 26.
Other references as above.

III. From his Return to Canaan to his Death.
Humphrey, Sacred Hist., chap. 25.
Other references same as above.

NOTES.

I. From his Birth to his Flight (74 Years).

The Record of this Period. Gen. 25: 21; 27: 40.

Outline.

1. *The Oracle at his Birth.* Gen. 25: 23; Mal. 1: 2–3; Rom. 9: 11–13. (See above.)
2. *Jacob's Occupation.* Gen. 25: 27.
3. *The Purchase of the Birthright.* Gen. 25: 29–34. (See above.)
4. *Supplants Esau.* Gen. 27: 1–40. (See above.)

II. From his Flight to his Return to Canaan. Gen. 27: 41; 32: 1-32.

This period extends over about twenty years, and may be divided into three stages: 1. *His Flight from Beersheba;* 2. *His Exile in Padan-aram;* 3. *His Return.* Let us study the events recorded in each stage.

1. *His Flight.*
   (1) Urged by his mother. 27: 41–46. Why? To what place?
   (2) Isaac's charge to Jacob. 28: 1–6. Give the points in this address of Isaac.
   (3) Jacob's first theophany, at Luz, fifty miles from Beersheba. 28: 10–22. Points in this theophany:—
      (*a*) Communication opened between Jehovah and Jacob. v. 12. Significance.
      (*b*) Jacob's heirship to the covenant declared. v. 13.
      (*c*) Promise concerning the spiritual seed greatly enlarged. 14.
      (*d*) The Messianic promise repeated. v. 14.

SECOND PERIOD. 71

(e) Jehovah's presence and blessing promised. v. 15.
(f) Impression made upon Jacob. 16–22.
(g) Typical nature of this theophany. "It teaches the people of God that a way of holy fellowship and communion is established between God and man. The angels are the ministers of grace, passing to and fro, and bringing help in every time of need to God's chosen ones. But it was reserved for Christ to unfold its most profound meaning." John 1: 51.
(4) Jacob's arrival at the house of Laban. 29: 1–13. Distance from Beersheba to Padanaram about 450 miles.—*II.* Laban? His family and circumstances?

2. *His Exile.* About twenty years. Jacob now 77 years old, a little past middle life.
(1) Engages to serve Laban seven years for Rachel. 15–20.
(2) At the end of seven years Jacob is deceived by Laban and Leah given him instead of Rachel. 21–25.
(3) Serves seven other years for Rachel. 27–30.
(4) The unhappiness in the family of Jacob. The family history traceable in the names of the children. 29: 31–35 and 30: 1–24. Polygamy one cause of this unhappiness.
(5) Serves Laban six years more for his cattle. 30: 25–43. Jacob's wealth. v. 43.

3. *His Return.*
(1) The reasons for his return, two:—
(a) The jealousy of Laban and his sons. 31: 1–2.

(b) The command of God. v. 3. This command given in a theophany (11-13), the second theophany to Jacob.
(2) Jacob's address to his wives. vs. 4-17.
(3) Jacob's secret departure. 17-21.
(4) Laban's pursuit; overtakes Jacob at Gilead; Laban's dream. 22-25.
(5) The interview between Jacob and Laban. The stolen gods. These gods were "teraphim, small images worshiped in the family and consulted as oracles, not unlike the penates, or household gods of the Romans." This incident shows the danger from idolatry to which Jacob and his family were exposed in Padan-aram. The quarrel. The covenant. 25-55.
(6) Mahanaim (two hosts). "One host for himself and the other pitched near by for the angels. The warlike terms, God's host and Mahanaim, point to an outstanding controversy, an impending conflict, and a sure protection."—*H.*
(7) Preparation to meet Esau.
   (a) The messengers and their report. 32: 3-6.
   (b) Divides his caravan into two companies. 7-8.
   (c) Prays. vs. 9-12. This prayer exceedingly comprehensive and beautiful.

ANALYSIS.

   (aa) The invocation. v. 9.
   (bb) Confession. v. 10 (first half).
   (cc) Thankful acknowledgment. v. 10 (second part).
   (dd) Supplication. v. 11.
   (ee) The plea. v. 12.
   (d) Sends a present to Esau.

SECOND PERIOD. 73

(8) Conveys his family and possessions across the Jabbok, remaining himself alone on the farther shore.
(9) Peniel. 32 : 24–32. Theophany. Doubtless unexplained mysteries here, and yet the theophany one of very great interest. It took place at night when Jacob was alone on the bank of the Jabbok. Let us first ascertain the facts and then consider the interpretation.

THE FACTS.

(a) "There wrestled a man with him until the breaking of the day."
(b) The "man" not prevailing, "touched the hollow of Jacob's thigh," dislocating it.
(c) The "man" then proposed to leave Jacob.
(d) But now Jacob becomes the suppliant and importunately and persistently implores his blessing.
(e) Jacob's prayer answered and his name changed to Israel.

INTERPRETATION.

(a) The "man" who wrestled with Jacob was God in the form of man. v. 30; Hos. 12 : 3–4.
(b) The transaction here recorded took place between God and Jacob only. Jacob was here alone with God.
(c) The narrative records a *real* struggle, not a hallucination, vision, or dream.
(d) In the first part of this struggle God wrestles with Jacob. The physical struggle, mysterious as it was, doubtless typified

the inner spiritual struggle. God was moving mightily upon Jacob's heart. John 16:8–11. Not until the miraculous touch did God prevail. Then conviction was complete, and all resistance ended.

(e) In the second stage of the struggle Jacob wrestles with God. The awakened, humbled, convicted sinner realizes that God is his only hope. He therefore clings to him with all the earnestness and importunity of despair. Hos. 12:4.

(f) God bestows the blessing. Jacob has prevailed, and in token of this fact his name changed to Israel. This blessing evidently the blessing of regeneration. Henceforth Jacob is a changed man. The old Jacob was tricky, deceitful, cowardly. The new Israel is open, frank, courageous.

III. From his Return to Canaan (Crossing Jabbok) to his Death.

The biography of Jacob from his return to Canaan to his death may be distributed into three periods:

1. *His Journey from Jabbok to Hebron* (10 years). Principal events:

(1) Meeting Esau. 33:1–15.
(2) Succoth. 33:17.
(3) Shechem. 33:18–20 and chap. 34.
(4) Bethel. (a) God's command. 35:1. (b) Preparation for removal. 2–4. (c) The journey. v. 5. (d) Arrival and altar. 6–7. (e) Another theophany. 9–12.
5) Death of Rachel. vs. 16–20.

2. *Sojourn in Hebron* (about 22 years).
Principal events:
   (1) The sale of Joseph. 37:23-28.
   (2) Famine in Canaan. 42:1.
   (3) Sends his ten sons to Egypt to buy corn. 42: 2-3.
   (4) Their return and report. 42:29-38.
   (5) Sends his sons the second time, including Benjamin. 43:1-14.
   (6) Journey of Jacob to Egypt. 46:1.
   (7) The theophany at Beersheba. 46:1-4.
3. *Dwells in Egypt until his Death* (17 years).
   (1) Who went to Egypt? Gen. 46:8-27.
   (2) The meeting of Jacob and Joseph. vs. 28-34.
   (3) The presentation of Jacob to Pharaoh. 47:1-10.
   (4) Settlement in Goshen. v. 27.
   (5) Adoption of Manasseh and Ephraim. Chap. 48.
   (6) Prophesies concerning his sons. Last scene in a memorable life. A dying old man, his twelve sons gathered at his bedside, all full grown, mature men. Jacob, the father, is the chief representative of the chosen seed, and head of the visible church, and now is about to speak as a prophet of God.
      (*a*) Address to all. 49:1-2.
      (*b*) Jacob begins with Reuben, doubtless because Reuben was the first-born, and as such entitled to the birthright. (Recall the elements of the birthright.) This birthright Reuben had forfeited by his sin, recorded in Gen. 35:22.
      (*c*) Distribution of the birthright. (*aa*) Chieftainship to Judah. (*bb*) Double portion

to Joseph. (cc) Priesthood to Levi.
(d) Simeon and Levi. vs. 5–7. This oracle was fulfilled when Simeon received in Canaan, not an independent inheritance, but a few scattered cities in Judah's lot (1 Chron. 4:27), and to Levi were awarded forty-eight cities in different districts. Behold how lasting and blighting the effects of sin!
(e) Judah 8:12. This the most interesting and important of all. Elements: (aa) Unchallenged supremacy over his brethren. v. 8—the chieftainship which Reuben had forfeited. (bb) He will maintain his supremacy by force of arms, his hand in the neck of his enemies, the lion tribe. (cc) This supremacy shall continue until Shiloh come. This raises a question of great interest : Who is Shiloh? Some say a term pointing to Solomon; others, a restful, a peaceful age—impersonal ; others, local, referring to a town of that name in Canaan—till he shall come to Shiloh. Neither satisfactory. The great body of interpreters, both Jewish and Christian, apply the title to the Messiah. Christ the true Shiloh, or Rest. This the fourth Messianic promise, the preceding being Gen. 3:15; Gen. 9:26; 12:3. (dd) Great temporal blessings. 11–12.
(f) Prophecies concerning the six subordinate tribes (Zebulon, Issachar, Dan, Gad, Asher, Naphtali). 13–21. "These prophecies, so brief and enigmatical as to defy at this distant time, anything like

a really discriminating application or a trustworthy historical vindication." In reference to the question as to whether history vindicates Jacob as a prophet it has been truly said, "The six tribes which are most prominent in Jacob's address are most prominent also in the subsequent history, whereas the six tribes which are put in the background by Jacob occupy the background in the history."—*Humphrey.*

(*g*) Jacob's charge concerning his burial. 28–32. Do all these prophecies and Jacob's charge concerning his burial presuppose a return to Canaan?

(7) Death, Mourning, Embalming. Burial. Age. 49:33, and 50:1–13.

4. *Question: Why were the chosen seed removed to Egypt?* The following are some of the reasons suggested by Dr. Humphrey:

(1) To prevent the intermarriage of the Israelites and heathen, leading to a fusion of races; God's plan was to keep the chosen seed separate. Danger in Canaan? Simeon and Judah? Why no danger in Egypt? 43:32; 46:34. Also, the Hebrews slew for food and sacrifice the animals worshiped by the Egyptians. Ex. 7:26.

(2) The expansion and consolidation of the chosen seed into a nation was conditioned on their expatriation. The problem to be solved was, how to develop the twelve patriarchs into a great people in such a manner as to secure their organic unity as one commonwealth, and to preserve their organic diversity as twelve

tribes. Difficulties of doing this in Canaan? How attained in Egypt?

(3) The relations of the Hebrews to their neighbors in Canaan were exceedingly critical. Both nations growing. If they remain separate nations one must give way or be subjugated.

(4) The plan of Providence in this exile contemplated a change in the habits of the people suited to their destiny as an exalted theocratic nation. Now this thorough transformation of simple nomads into husbandmen, architects, engineers, weavers, artists, and jewelers could scarcely have been effected in Canaan. Egypt became, on a large scale, a school of industry and the arts for the Hebrews. The discipline was severe, but the education was thorough.

(5) By the removal of the chosen seed into Egypt the kingdom of God was transplanted for a season into the heart of a great pagan empire. Ex. 7:5; Ez. 39:21.

This history affords a very remarkable illustration of the truth, *God sovereign* and *man free*. We have revealed in Genesis 15:13 the sovereign purpose of God. Behold the wonderful manner of its fulfillment! "The narrative brings before us also the many persons, in many lands, through whose instrumentality the divine purpose was brought about. Isaac, Rebekah, Esau, Jacob, in Canaan; Laban, Leah, and Rachel, in Mesopotamia; Reuben, Judah, and the Ishmaelitish merchants in Dothan; Potiphar and his wife, the butler, the baker, and Pharaoh in Egypt, appear one by one in the story. Each of them in his turn wove his own separate thread into the tapestry, and stepped aside to give place to another, knowing nothing of the rare and luminous device, even the divine ideal, which was gradually coming out on the hidden side of the canvas."—*H.*, pp. 388–9. Did God accomplish his purpose? How? Was man free?

SECTION 5. JOSEPH.

GEN. 30:22-24; 33:2; CHAPS. 37 TO 49.

OUTLINE.

I. **His Early Life.**
Humphrey, Sacred Hist., chap. 25.
Geikie, Hours, chap. 24.
Dods, Genesis.
Blaikie, Manual, sec. 4.

II. **In Potiphar's House.**
Humphrey, Sacred Hist., chap. 26.
Other references same as above.

III. **In Prison.**
Same references.

IV. **Viceroy of Egypt.**
Same references.

NOTES.

I. **Joseph's Early Life (17 Years).**

1. *His Birth.* Gen. 30: 22–24. Rachel, the favorite wife of Jacob. Bearing upon the treatment Joseph would receive? Jacob removed from Padan-aram while Joseph was yet

an infant (v. 25). Joseph's early life spent in Canaan, and *after* Jacob's conversion and the putting away of all false gods.
2. *The Partiality Shown by his Father.* 33:2; 37:3.
3. *Hated of his Brethren.* 37:4.
4. *Joseph's Dream.* 37:5–11.
5. *Sale to the Midianites.* 37:12–28. "Midian and Medan were sons of Keturah—cousins, therefore, of Ishmael, and not very distantly related to Joseph. The names Ishmaelite and Midianite may have been interchangeable, either because the caravan was composed of men from both tribes; or, more probably, because the term Ishmaelite, as a geographical or professional name, comprehended that of Midian."—*Dods.*

II. In Potiphar's House.

1. *Sold by the Midianites to Potiphar.* 37:36 and 39:1. "Potiphar was probably at the head of what may be called the Egyptian State Police, which formed one of the corps of the army, though largely employed in civil duties."— *Geikie.*
2. *The Blessing of God upon Him.* 39:2–3.
3. *His Promotion.* vs. 4–6.
4. *Cast into Prison on a False Charge.* 39:7–20. "The crime laid to his charge, under the laws of Egypt, was punishable with 1,000 blows. A horrible death."—*Humphrey.*

III. In Prison:

1. *At First Very Harshly Treated.* Ps. 105:18.
2. *Promoted.* 39:21–23. Made underwarden of the prison. Why? vs. 21 and 23.

3. *Interprets the Dreams of Pharaoh's Butler and Baker.* Chap. 40. The chief butler was the King's cup-bearer. He had the responsible duty of protecting the King's life from poison. The King drank nothing except from the hand of this cup-bearer. His office, therefore, gave him constant and confidential access to Pharaoh. The chief baker had not only to oversee the due supply of the court with the endless cakes and bake-meats in which Egyptians delighted, but to take care they were not tampered with for traitorous use.—*Geikie.* Their dreams? The interpretation? How Joseph was enabled to interpret them?

4. *Interprets Pharaoh's Dream.* 41 : 1–37.

(1) Pharaoh's dream?

(2) The wise men of Egypt? The magicians and wise men were chosen from the sacred order. " Every large temple had its college of priests, over whom one presided as chief. From among the high priests the foremost men were chosen as a hierarchy for all Egypt, and of these a selected number, the most eminent in dignity, lived in the royal palace to attend the King; one selected from them acting as sovereign pontiff for all Egypt. When, however, weighty questions, such as that of these dreams, had to be solved, this standing council of high ecclesiastics, which seems to have been twenty in number, was augmented by the heads of the great temples throughout the country, and the united body was invited to aid the King in his perplexity. They did not affect to speak by direct inspiration in

giving their interpretations, but confined themselves to consulting their holy books and to performing magical rites."—*Geikie.*
(3) Joseph sent for. By whom? Why? vs. 9–13.
(4) Preparations for meeting Pharaoh. "No one could appear before the majesty of Egypt unless he were in all respects ceremonially clean."
(5) The interpretation. 15–32.
(6) Joseph's advice to Pharaoh. 33–36.

IV. **Viceroy of Egypt.**
1. *His Appointment and Rank.* 41 : 39–44. Now 30 years old. He was sold into Egypt at the age of 17. "According to Usher's Chronology, his stewardship in Potiphar's house occupied less than a year, and his imprisonment lasted twelve years. He rose suddenly from the condition of a prisoner to the dignity of the grand vizier."
2. *His Preparation for the High Position.*
    (1) His early training, by his father, in piety. This the source in him of incorruptible purity and integrity.
    (2) The discipline of adversity and suffering, giving spiritual purification. Ps. 105 : 17–19. The arrogance of the stripling had disappeared from the chastened man.
    (3) His administrative ability had been partially developed by his experience, as was seen in Potiphar's house, and as the deputy warden in prison.
    (4) The blessing and guidance of God.—*H.*
3. *His Marriage.* v. 45. His two sons. vs. 50–52.
4. *Provision for the Famine.* 41 : 46–49.

5. *The Famine Begins.* 41 : 53–57.
6. *Joseph's First Meeting with his Brethren.* 42 : 1–28.
   (1) Joseph recognizes his brethren. v. 7.
   (2) They do not recognize him. Why not?
   (3) Joseph's harsh treatment of his brethren. Why? Doubtless "he intended to rebuke their cruelty in selling him as a slave. But it is evident that he began very early to consider the propriety of removing his father's whole family to Egypt in order to preserve them alive through the famine. But before doing that he must subject the disposition of his brothers to repeated and decisive tests. He must be assured that they were not in the same temper that led some of them, twenty-two years before, to desire to kill him, and all of them to sell him into slavery." What were their feelings toward him? Would they repeat their deception upon their father? How did they feel toward Benjamin? Were they at peace among themselves? Would it be safe to remove them to Egypt?—*Humphrey.* Hence the severe tests.
7. *The Second Meeting with his Brethren.* 43 : 15–34 and 44 : 1–34.
8. *Joseph and his Brethren.* 45 : 1–15.
   (1) Joseph reveals himself. v. 1.
   (2) Effect upon his brethren. v. 3.
   (3) Address to his brethren. 3–13.
   (4) The clew to Joseph's history. vs. 7–8.
9. *Joseph Removes his Father and Brethren to Egypt.* 45 : 16–28.
10. *Settles Them in Goshen and Nourishes Them.* 48 : 1–12.

11. *Joseph's Administration during the Famine.* 47: 13-26. For his administration Joseph has been criticised. It is proper to say in answer, that until more is known of how far Joseph acted under Pharaoh, and of the condition of the peasantry of Egypt before and after the famine, the criticism is not fair.
12. *His Death.* 50: 24-26.
   (1) His faith (v. 24); (2) oath exacted of his brethren (v. 25); (3) embalmed (v. 26).
13. *Joseph's Character and Place in History.*

SECTION 6. THE BONDAGE.

Exodus 1, 10 and 11.

OUTLINE.

I. Israel in Egypt.
Gibson, Mosaic Era, chap. 1.
Humphrey, Sacred Hist., chap. 27.
Geikie, Hours, chap. 3.

II. The Deliverer—Moses.
Gibson, Mosaic Era, chap. 2.
Humphrey, Sacred Hist., chap. 29.
Geikie, Hours, chap. 4.

III. The Preparation of the People for Deliverance.
Gibson, Mosaic Era, chap. 2.
Humphrey, Sacred Hist., chap. 28.
Geikie, Hours, chap. 3.

IV. From Midian to Egypt.
Same authors.

V. Moses before Pharaoh.

Gibson, Mosaic Era, chap. 3.
Humphrey, Sacred Hist., chap. 30.
Blaikie, Manual, p. 113.

VI. General View of the Plagues.

Dr. W. W. Moore, in *Union Seminary Magazine*, November and December, 1891.
Geikie, Hours, chap. 5.
Other references same as above.

VII. The First Nine Plagues.

Same references.

NOTES.

I. Israel in Egypt. Chap. 1.

1. *Condition of Jews in Egypt up to the Change of Dynasty.* vs. 1–7.
2. *Pharaoh's First Effort at Suppression.* Why? vs. 8–10. Method? 11–14.
3. *Pharaoh's Second Effort at Suppression.* Infanticide. vs. 15–22. All this foretold. Gen. 15:13. But why did it enter into the divine plan for Israel to be thus afflicted? The answer may be found in Gen. 46:3.

II. The Deliverer—Moses.

1. *His Family.* Tribe (6:16–20); parents (6:20; Heb. 11:23); brother? sister?
2. *His Infancy.* Born under the royal edict for the extermination of all male children. But this very edict the means of his transfer to Pharaoh's court and his training in all the learning of the Egyptians. Note how God makes even the wrath of man to praise him.

3. *The Rescue and Adoption.* vs. 5-10. See what a wonderful concurrence of events, the floating of the ark to the very spot where Pharaoh's daughter came, and at the very time she came, the cry of the infant so as to fall on her ear and move her sympathy. Was this a special providence? The adoption? The provision for taking care of the babe?

4. *Forty Years' Training in Egypt.* Acts 7:22. "No country in these early ages was so far advanced in civilization as Egypt; none could boast so grand a history; such far-reaching power; such splendor of architecture; such knowledge of arts and sciences; such royal magnificence in its government or such accumulation of wealth in its national treasury and in the hands of its nobles and priests."—*Geikie's Hours, p. 43.* Every opportunity all this offered Moses enjoyed. Bearing of such a training as he would thus receive upon his great mission? Doubtless also in his tender years he received the training of a pious mother. Hence Heb. 11:24-26.

5. *His Espousal of the Cause of the People.* 2:11-12; Acts 7:23-25.

6. *Forty Years in the Desert of Midian.* Why he left Egypt. 2:14-15. Now began another kind of training. "Egypt was a good place for a course in arts, but it was no place for theology. The rocks of the desert make a far better divinity hall than the temples of Heliopolis. To become truly acquainted with God a man must be much alone."—*Gibson.* Eighty years of training for his life work of forty

SECOND PERIOD.

years! Yet all the time the cruel oppression was going on.

7. *Moses' Call.* 3:1-10. This a theophany, the first that had appeared since Jacob was at Beersheba, nearly four hundred years before; the first, also, that had assumed the form of a flame since the days of Abraham. Gen. 15:17.

THE THEOPHANY OF THE BURNING BUSH.

(1) The name applied to the Almighty in this revelation. v. 2; v. 6; v. 7; v. 14. Significance of these names?

(2) The relation which this God sustains to his people. vs. 15-16. See here the perpetuity of the Abrahamic covenant. Four hundred years had elapsed since that covenant had been given. Moreover, this covenant is mentioned as the basis of the proposed deliverance. See again here, in the light of these facts, the meaning of Gen. 17:7—"to be a God unto thee and thy seed after thee."

(3) The call. v. 10.

(4) The commission. 14-22. In these verses the Lord reveals unto Moses the authority under which he was to act (v. 14); the messages he was to bear, to Hebrews (vs. 15-17), to Pharaoh (v. 18), and foretells the results (19-22).

(5) Moses' objections overruled.
    First objection. v. 11. Answer. v. 12.
    Second objection. 4:1. Answer. 4:2-9.
    (Three signs.)
    Third objection. v. 10. Answer. vs. 11-12.
    Fourth objection. v. 13. Answer. vs. 14-17.

(6) Moses' credentials.
  (a) The miracle of the rod. vs. 2–5. To appreciate this, remember that the serpent was an emblem of royalty in Egypt. This miracle a sign that the King of Egypt would be as harmless in his hand as his own shepherd's staff, and that he should have the complete mastery over Pharaoh.
  (b) The miracle of the leprous hand. vs. 6–8. This leprous hand represented the condition of the people of Israel. In their degraded and despised estate, they were as a community of lepers; but by the restoring of the leprous hand God gave to Moses a sign of his power to save.
  (c) The miracle of turning the water into blood. v. 9. The Nile was the life and strength and source of all the greatness of Egypt, and accordingly was worshiped as the great god of Egypt; but how easily is this god put to shame before Jehovah! Thus God has prepared and equipped the deliverer.

III. The Preparation of the People for Deliverance
1. *The Severity of the Oppression.* 2: 23.
2. *The Yearning and Faith of the People.* 4: 31. Brought by the providence of God to a sense of their humiliation and need; and led, in some measure, to look unto God for deliverance and submit themselves to his guidance.

IV. From Midian to Egypt.
1. *The Divine Command.* 4: 19 and 23.
2. *Moses' Obedience.* v. 20.

SECOND PERIOD. 89

3. *The Meeting of Moses and Aaron.* 27–28.
4. *Moses and Aaron Declare their Mission to the Elders.* 29–31.

V. **Moses before Pharaoh.**

1. *Presents the Demand of God.* 5 : 1 and 3. "The request was put in this form to give a religious aspect to the conflict, to show that it was a struggle not merely between Pharaoh and Moses, but between the god of Egypt, whom Pharaoh represented, and the God of Israel. Both Pharaoh and Moses understood quite well that if the request was once granted, Pharaoh's authority over the people would be entirely at an end. During the contest, Pharaoh seems to have been residing at the royal city of Zoan, near Goshen."—*Blaikie.*
2. *Pharaoh's Reply.* vs. 2, 4, 5.
3. *The Result of this Interview.* 6–21.
4. *Moses' Prayer.* 22–23.
5. *The Answer.* 6 : 1–8.
6. *The Demand Repeated before Pharaoh and Accompanied by Supernatural Proof of Moses' Divine Commission.* 6 : 28 ; 7 : 13. The obstinate refusal of Pharaoh to grant the demand of God led to the visitation upon Egypt of the plagues, or divine judgments.

VI. **General View of the Plagues.**

1. *Number—ten; viz.:* (1) *Blood,* (2) *Frogs,* (3) *Lice,* (4) *Flies,* (5) *Murrain,* (6) *Boils,* (7) *Hail,* (8) *Locusts,* (9) *Darkness,* (10) *Death of the First-born.*
2. *These without Exception Miracles.* "The word miracle is here used to describe not only a

supernatural event, but a wonder wrought by God through the instrumentality of man." Acts 2 : 22. "In this sense of the word, no miracle was done from the creation to the age of Moses, a period of 2,500 years. . . . . Through all these early ages the Almighty revealed his being and will by visions, from which the period derives the name of the theophanic era. The age of miracles, as distinguished from theophanies, began with Moses. . . . . Here, then, was the beginning of miracles in the history of redemption."—*Humphrey*, 441–2.

3. *These Miracles must be Distinguished from the Jugglery of the Egyptians.* "The opinion concerning the feats of the magicians best supported by the Scriptures and most commonly received is, that the magicians were adepts in legerdemain, and their enchantments were simply due to their cleverness in their profession."—*Humphrey, p.* 449.

4. *Intervals.* " Another common misapprehension in regard to the plagues is that they followed each other in rapid succession. The fact is, that they fell at intervals of a month or more, with the exception of the last two, which came close together." From Ex. 5:11–12 and 9: 31–32, it is evident " nearly a year elapsed between the opening of the contest and the plague of hail. The whole series of plagues then must have extended over a period of about ten months."—*Rev. Dr. Moore, U. S. Mag., Nov.,* 1891.

5. *Natural Basis.* The most of these miracles have a natural basis in the familiar phenomena of Egypt. This fact has been urged by rationalists to explain away the miraculous in these plagues. "But then it must not be forgotten that they came at the word of Moses and went at the word of Moses, one after another, and at the word of Moses God would spare the land of Goshen where Israel lived."—*Gibson.*

6. *Polytheism.* "The fundamental assumption underlying the following interpretation of the ten plagues is, that the religion of Egypt was at this time a gross and degraded Polytheism. Of the correctness of this assumption there can be no doubt. . . . Beast, and reptile, and insect, sun, and soil, and river—these were the gods of Egypt, and against these were the miraculous plagues directed in order to teach the great lesson that there is no god but God."— *Ex.* 7 : 5 ; *Ex.* 7 : 17 ; *Ex.* 8 : 22. *Dr. W. W. Moore, U. S. Mag.,* 1891.

7. *The Design of the Plagues.*

(1) As to Israel. They could scarcely fail to inspire the bondmen with faith in the promise and power of God to break their chains.— *Humphrey.*

(2) As to Egypt. "And against all the gods of Egypt I will execute judgment."—*Ex.* 12 : 12.

(3) As to God himself. To reveal himself as the only true God that he might be glorified.

VII. The First Nine Plagues:

First Plague. Blood. 7 : 14–25. Natural basis. The reddish color of the water of the Nile at the period of the overflow. "But the overflow occurred in July, whereas the plague of blood took place in February."—*Humphrey.* Moreover, at the word of Moses the water became blood. See also v. 21. Idolatry? Nile worship. Effect upon Pharaoh? v. 23. Magicians? v. 22. Duration? v. 25.

The Second Plague. Frogs. 8: 1–15. The warning? The plague? The Magicians? The Effect upon Pharaoh? v. 8. Removed? 9–14. Result? v. 15. Frog worship. "It is by no means so easy for us to explain the worship of frogs as it is to explain the worship of the Nile. Of the fact there can be no question. Brugsch informs us that a female deity, with a frog's head, named Heka, was worshiped in the district of Sah. 'Lepsius has shown that the frog was connected with the most ancient form of nature worship in Egypt.' 'It was embalmed and honored with burial at Thebes.'"—*Moore, as above.*

Third Plague. Lice. 8: 16–19. No warning. The plague? The magicians? Idolatry? "The soil of Egypt was as sacred as everything else in the valley of the Nile, for it was worshiped as Seb, father of the gods. But now it was to be defiled, by its very dust seeming to turn into noisome pests."—*Geikie's Hours, p.* 86. Effect upon Pharaoh? v. 19.

Fourth Plague. Flies. 8: 20–32. The warning? 20–21. The plague? v. 24. "The word rendered 'swarms of flies' in our version should have been rendered 'beetle'."—*Moore.* Natural basis? Supernatural? A new supernatural element here for the first time appears. v. 22. Idolatry? "This insect was sculptured on every monument, painted on every tomb, and on every mummy chest, engraved on gems, worn round the neck as an amulet, and honored in ten thousand images of every size and of all material. That it, among other insects, should be multiplied into a plague, was a blow at idolatry that would come home to all."— *Geikie.* Effect upon Pharaoh? Proposes two compromises:

(a) In the land. v. 25. Ans. vs. 26–27.
(b) Not very far away. v. 28.
    Plague removed? vs. 29–31. Result? v. 32.

Fifth Plague. Murrain. 9:1–7. The warning? vs. 1–3. Also time given to consider. v. 5. The plague? Natural basis? "Murrain is even yet not uncommon in Egypt and sometimes is very fatal."—*Geikie.* Supernatural? vs. 4–5. Idolatry? "Not only frogs and beetles, but many other insects and reptiles and animals were worshiped as divine, and the penalty of killing one of these sacred brutes was death. In like manner, dogs, apes, hawks, hippopotami, crocodiles, sheep, goats and cows were reverenced. In some cases the animal was believed to be the actual incarnation of the god, *e. g.*, the bull Apis at Memphis; the bull Mnevis at Heliopolis, and the goat Khem at Medes. The most interesting form of this animal cult was the worship of Apis, who was regarded as the incarnation of Ptah."—*Dr. Moore, as above.* Effect upon Pharaoh? v. 7.

Sixth Plague. Boils. 9:8–12. No warning. The plague? Religious aspect? "In various Egyptian towns sacred to Set or Typhon, the god of Evil. . . . Red haired and light complexioned men, and as such, foreigners, perhaps often Hebrews, were yearly offered in sacrifice to this idol. After being burned alive on a high altar, their ashes were scattered in the air by the priests, in the belief that they would avert evil from all parts whither they were blown. But even the ashes thrown into the air by Moses, instead of carrying blessing with them, fell everywhere in a rain of blains and boils on the people and even on the cattle which the murrain had spared."—*Geikie, p. 89.* The Magicians? v. 11. Effect upon Pharaoh? v. 12.

Seventh Plague. Hail. 9:13-35. The warning? vs. 13-21. The plague? vs. 22-26. "Such a phenomenon was unheard of, for though thunder and hail are not unknown in Egypt in spring, they are rarely severe. How must it have shocked a nation so devout toward its gods, to find that the waters, the earth, and the air, the growth of the fields, the cattle, and even their own persons, all under the care of a host of divinities, were yet in succession smitten by a power against which their protectors were impotent." Effect upon Pharaoh? 27-28. Plague removed. v. 33. Result? 34-35.

Eighth Plague. Locusts. 10:1-20. The Warning? 1-6. Effect? 7-11. The Plague? 12-15. Effect upon Pharaoh? 16-17. Removed? 18-19. Result? 20.

Ninth Plague. Darkness. 10:21-29. No Warning. The Plague? 21-23. "A physical phenomenon frequent in Egypt, though of less intensity, may possibly illustrate the agency divinely used to produce this result. A hot wind known as the

Chamsin blows from the equator, in Africa, towards the north, in April, or between March and May. . . . It is always attended with a thickness of the air, through which the sun sheds only at best a dim yellow light; even this passing in many cases into complete darkness."—*Geikie*. "What then? Do these facts prove that the plague of darkness inflicted by Moses was a merely natural phenomenon? By no means."—*Moore*. Cf. v. 22–24. Idolatry? The sun was the supreme god of Egypt, and he, too, now veils himself, or is veiled before Jehovah. Effect upon Pharaoh? 24.

REVIEW CHART OF THE SECOND PERIOD.

SEC. 1. Abraham.

(Introductory.)

    I. Before the Giving of the Covenant.
    II. The Covenant.
    III. After the giving of the Covenant.
    IV. The Prominence of Abraham in the Bible.

SEC. 2. Isaac.

    I. From his Birth to his Marriage.
    II. From his Marriage to his Death.

SEC. 3. Jacob and Esau.

(Introductory.)

    I. The Difference between Jacob and Esau.
    II. The Sale of the Birthright.
    III. Jacob Supplants Esau.

SEC. 4. Jacob.

    I. From his Birth to his Flight.
    II. From his Flight to his Return to Canaan.
    III. From his Return to Canaan to his Death.

SEC. 5. Joseph.

    I. His Early History.
    II. In Potiphar's House.
    III. In Prison.
    IV. Viceroy of Egypt.

SEC. 6. The Bondage.

    I. Israel in Egypt.
    II. The Deliverer—Moses.
    III. The Preparation of the People for Deliverance.
    IV. From Midian to Egypt.
    V. Moses before Pharaoh.
    VI. General View of the Plagues.
    VII. The First Nine Plagues.

QUESTIONS ON THE PERIOD.   TOPICS FOR SPECIAL STUDY.

4. What position does the Covenant hold in the history of Abraham.
5. What were the great features of the Abrahamic Covenant.
6. What were the principal events in the life of Isaac, and their importance?
7. Why was Jacob chosen as the heir of the Covenant?
8. What were the principal events in the life of Jacob?
9. What were the principal events in the life of Joseph?
10. What was the early history of Moses?
11. What were the characteristics of the first nine Plagues?
12. Trace the history and progress of redemption in this Period.

5. Jacob's Conversion.
6. Joseph's Administration.
7. The Plagues.
8. The Israelites and Egyptology.
9. The Length of Israel's Stay in Egypt.
10. The Characters of the Patriarchs.
11. The Messianic Promises.
12. God in the History of the Period.

THIRD PERIOD.

THE WANDERINGS. FROM THE EXODUS TO
THE SETTLEMENT IN CANAAN. 91 YEARS.

SECTION 1. THE TENTH PLAGUE.

OUTLINE.

(Introductory.)
I. The Plague.
Gibson, Mosaic Era, chap. 4.
Humphrey, Sacred Hist., chap. 32.
Geikie, Hours, chap. 6.
Butler's Bible Work, Exodus.

II. The Passover.
Same references.

III. The Exodus.
Same references.

NOTES.

Introductory.
(1) This plague the culmination of the series. "The nine were preliminary to the tenth, and in the nature of warnings; the tenth was the work of final judgment."—*Humphrey.*

(2) Importance indicated by the space given it— two whole chapters.

(3) These two chapters record two distinct events: a Plague and a Passover, a Destruction and a Salvation. Hence the following divisions:

I. The Plague.

1. *What it Was.* Death of first-born.
2. *Upon Whom it Fell.* 11 : 4–5.
3. *Characteristics.*
    (1) Prophesied four days before.
    (2) Thoroughly supernatural. "Unlike most of the preceding wonders, the destruction of the oldest son was not a calamity indigenous to the country under a form intensely aggravated by the Almighty; but it was altogether a strange terror never before inflicted, never since repeated."—*Humphrey, p.* 463.
    (3) Time—midnight. 11 : 4.
    (4) Wrought by Jehovah himself. 11 : 4.
4. *Relation to Idolatry.* 12 : 12 ; Numb. 33 : 4. "The true explanation in this case is that in smiting the first-born of all living beings, man and beast, God smote the objects of Egyptian worship."—*B. Bible Work.* But especially was this blow severe upon Pharaoh, and through him the national idolatry. "For thus to abase the Pharaoh was to degrade national idolatry in his person, for he was himself the incarnation of the great sun-god Ra."—*Geikie.*
5. *Overwhelming Effect.* 12 : 30–33.

II. The Passover.

This word not only expresses the fact of Israel's deliverance from the Tenth Plague, but includes also the *method* of the deliverance.

1. *The Plan of Protection Revealed by Jehovah.* 12: 3-7, and 21-23.
2. *Meaning of the Passover.*
    (1) It was a commemorative institution. 12: 14.
    (2) It was a teaching ordinance. "The doctrine taught is salvation by the shedding of blood." Ex. 12: 13 and 23.
    (3) It was a sacrifice. Ex. 12: 27; Deut. 16: 2-6.
    (4) It was also a sacrament. One of the two sacraments of the Old Testament.

    Elements of a Sacrament:
    (a) Divine appointment. God's command.
    (b) Sacramental sign. Here lamb slain.
    (c) Sacramental action. Here eating the flesh, etc.
    (d) Benefit signified. Here redemption.
    (5) It was a typical institution. 1 Cor. 5:7.
3. Result of the observance of the ordinance of the passover. Absolute safety.

III. The Exodus.

The last blow has been struck. Pharaoh has been subdued. Israel has been saved. God has been magnified.
1. *The Number of the Children of Israel who Went Out.* 12:37-38.
2. *The Manner of their Going Out.* Victorious, carrying with them great spoils. Concerning these spoils, observe:
    (1) The amount. Some idea may be formed from the contributions afterwards made to the Tabernacle. "The value of the gold and silver expended, and the building and appointments of the Tabernacle, are estimated by Canon

Cook at $1,165,550, by Arbuthnot and Bockh at somewhat less than a million dollars, and by Keil at three-quarters of a million in our money."—*H.*, 475.

(2) How obtained. 12:35–37 (Rev. Version.)

3. *The Victory of the Exodus.* By whom achieved. 13:9 and 14. Over whom? Pharaoh represented not only the world power, but heathenism and the seed of the serpent.

4. *The Victory to be Commemorated:*

(1) By the appointment of a new era. 12:2. "The Hebrews had been accustomed to begin the year with the month Tisri, corresponding very nearly with our October. The exodus occurred in the month Nisan, corresponding very nearly with our April, and by divine direction the year was thenceforth to begin at that time. According to Josephus this change determined the beginning of the ecclesiastical year only; the civil year began six months later, as before."

(2) By the redemption of the first-born. 13:15. "When a first-born child attained the age of a month the parents were required by the Levitical law to pay five shekels—say $2.50—into the sanctuary."

(3) By the sanctification of the first-born. "At the exodus God prepared the way for a sacerdotal order by setting apart for that purpose all the first-born sons of the twelve tribes. He declared that on the day when he smote the first-born of the Egyptians he separated unto himself all the first-born of Israel, both man and beast. Ex. 13:2. By this appointment the first-born male, both of man and

beast, was reserved for the altar—the former as the priest, the latter as the victim."—*II., p.* 471.

(4) By the annual observance of the feast of unleavened bread. 13:4–10.

5. *By the Exodus the nation has been born.*

SECTION 2. PHARAOH MANEPHTAH.

Humphrey's Sacred Hist., chap. 31.

The following outline is condensed from Dr. Humphrey's chapter entitled, "Pharaoh Manephtah":

1. *His Prominence.* This derived from many sources.
    (1) He stood in the illustrious line of the Pharaohs, who with the Ptolemys of a later age, were the Cæsars of Egypt. He was the son and immediate successor of Rameses the Great.
    (2) Egypt was an absolute monarchy of the oriental type of absolutism. The dignity of the kingdom was identical with the person of the king.
    (3) With the throne of his fathers, Manephtah inherited their divine honors. The name Pharaoh is derived from an Egyptian word signifying the sun. Wilkinson is of the opinion that the name was probably given in the earliest times to the Egyptian kings, because they claimed to be the chief on earth, as the sun is chief among the heavenly bodies; and afterwards, when this luminary became the object of idolatrous worship at Heliopolis,

it was the representative of their sun-god. "Son of the Sun" came to be the title of every Pharaoh, and Manephtah inherited this divine honor.

(4) Still further in the struggle on the Nile, the most formidable adversary of the true religion was not Pharaoh as a man, or as an official representative of Egypt, or as a king-god, but heathenism itself incarnate in his person, and endeavoring to strangle the church while in Egypt.

2. *The Temper of the King was Disclosed by his Treatment of the Request made of him by the Messengers of Jehovah.* Exodus 3:18; 5:1–2.

3. *The Hardening of Pharaoh's Heart. Prophesied* Ex. 4:21. The hardening mentioned twenty times in the history of the exodus, indicating the prominence given to the instance. In ten places ascribed to God. Ex. 4:21; 7:3; 9:12; 10:1, 20, 27; 11:10; 14:4, 8, 17. In four ascribed to Pharaoh. 8:15, 32; 9:34; 13:15. In six is impersonal. 7:13 (Revised ver.), 14, 22; 8:19; 9:7, 35. In attempting to explain this hardening it is important that we should hold fast the fact that evil is of man and that God bounds it most wisely and powerfully. Of the many views held concerning this hardening, the following seems to be the true one:

(1) The king had oppressed the chosen seed and had refused to let them go at God's command, even after the signs had confirmed the divine commission of Moses. Pharaoh had sinned, sinned grievously and inexcusably.

(2) God resolved to punish the cruel and disobedient monarch.
(3) The particular punishment awarded was hardness of heart.
(4) This sentence was carried into effect not only by the withdrawal of the restraints of providence and grace (cf. Rom. 1 : 24–32), but by placing the king in circumstances which, owing to his own perversity, served to harden his heart, although his heart ought to have been softened by them. Still further this hardening is to be contemplated under two aspects; under the one it was a grievous sin; under the other it was a severe punishment. As a sin, it was the act of Pharaoh; as a punishment, it was an act of God.

SECTION 3. THE ROUTE CHOSEN.
Ex. 13: 17–18.

Humphrey's Sacred Hist., chap. 33.

NOTES.

The Hebrews might have reached the promised land in forty days, going by the way of the south shore along the Mediterranean Sea, thence to Gaza and Hebron, the distance being less than 250 miles. . . . This near route was closed to the Hebrews by the hostility of the Philistines who dwelt about Gaza. Ex. 13 : 17. . . . Although a journey of a few months by the longer route might have brought them to their new home, yet, in punishment of their ignominious revolt at Kadesh in the matter of the spies, the Lord turned back the congregation into the wilderness thirty-eight years—forty years in all after the exodus. Reasons:

1. Time was given for the old and wayward race to pass from life and give place to a better generation.
2. It entered into the plan of Providence to afford to the Israelites time and opportunity for education in the law given from Sinai.
3. The heathen were not overlooked in the Providential design of the wandering. Ex. 15: 14–17; Josh. 2: 10–11.

SECTION 4. THE CLOUDY PILLAR.
Gen. 13: 21-22.

Humphrey's Sacred Hist., pp. 487–488.

NOTES.

1. *This a Theophany.* v. 21. Continuance? Neh. 9: 19.
2. *Design?* While the leading design of the pillar was to reveal Jehovah to the senses of the people by an open and perpetual vision of his majesty, it served other important purposes:
   (1) It shielded the people from the fierce rays of sun. Ps. 105: 39.
   (2) The motion of the cloud gave direction to their journey.
   (3) The movements of the wandering Israelites were controlled by the same phenomenon. It gave to the entire caravan the signal for moving or standing still.
   (4) The holy oracle was established within its folds. Ps. 99: 7.

The children of Israel have now gone out from Egypt; the route chosen, and the cloudy pillar guiding them. We now begin the study of the history of the wandering.

THIRD PERIOD. 105

SECTION 5. FROM SUCCOTH TO SINAI.

OUTLINE.

I. The Red Sea. Chaps. 14 and 15: 1-21.
II. Marah. 15: 22-26.
III. Wilderness of Sin. 16: 1.
IV. Meribah (Rephidim). 17: 1-6.
V. Smiting of Amalek. 17: 8-16.
VI. Jethro's Visit. 18: 1-27.

NOTES.

I. The Red Sea. Chaps. 14 and 15: 1-21.
   1. *The position of the Hebrews Taken by Divine Command.* 14: 1–2.
   2. *The Pursuit.* 3–9.
   3. *The Alarm of the Hebrews Allayed by Moses.* vs. 10–14.
   4. *The Passage of Israel.* vs. 15–22. Miracle?
   5. *Destruction of the Egyptians.* vs. 23–28.
   6. *Result.* vs. 29–31.
   7. *The Song of Moses.* 15: 1–21. (Analyze.)
   8. *The Importance of this Event in the History of Israel.*

II. Marah. 15: 22-26.
   1. *Murmuring.*
   2. *Water Sweetened.*
   3. *Comfort.* Condition? v. 26.

III. Wilderness of Sin. 16: 1.
   1. *Murmuring.* vs. 2–3.
   2. *Manna and Quails.* 12–36. Describe the manna. Its typical significance? John 6:

48–51. Rules for gathering? The Sabbath? How long continued? Miracle? Memorial kept.

IV. Meribah. (Rephidim). Why Called Meribah?
1. The Murmuring. 17 : 1–3.
2. Water. How procured. v. 6. Quantity? Ps. 78 : 15–16.

V. Smiting of Amalek. 17 : 8-16.
Amalek? (See Bible Dict.) Joshua mentioned for first time.
How the victory was won.
Curse upon Amalek.

VI. Jethro's Visit. The object of his Visit. 18: 1-6. The meeting with Moses. 7-12. His Counsel to Moses. 13-27.

SECTION 6. THE SINAITIC COVENANT.

OUTLINE.

(Introduction.)
Humphrey, MS. Notes of Lects.
Butler's Bible Work.

I. The Sinaitic Covenant Described.
Same references.

II. The Moral Law.
Dabney, Theology Lect. 30.
Gibson, Mosaic Era, chap. 6.
Humphrey, MS. Notes of Lects.
Butler's Bible Work.

III. The Ceremonial Law.
Humphrey, Preparing to Teach, p. 71–99.

Gibson, Mosaic Era, chaps. 7–15.
Butler's Bible Work.
Barrow, Companion to the Bible.
Barrow, Sacred Geog. and Antiq.
Geikie, Hours, chap. 10.
Hurlbut, Manual Bib. Geog., etc., p. 135.

IV. The Civil Law.

Humphrey, MS. Notes.
Butler's Bible Work.

NOTES.

Introduction.

This Covenant the fifth of the series: (1) Covenant of work, (2) Covenant of grace, (3) Covenant of forbearance, (4) Covenant with Abraham, (5) Covenant of Sinai.

1. *The Great Characteristic of this Covenant, Contains the Law of God.*
2. *The Relation of this Covenant to the Old Testament.* It is the central mass, the most important part and to which all the rest refers.
   (1) All before it introductory—*e. g.* Sacrifice, Priesthood, Ordinance of Worship (as the Sabbath), Government (patriarchal). All these had existed before by divine sanction and in a form suited to the condition and needs of the chosen people. The time had now come for developing and enlarging these ordinances, reducing them to the form of written law and adapting them to a larger application.
   (2) All subsequent history is the unfolding of this law; reveals its application, meaning and

working. The Old Testament may, therefore, be divided into three parts:
   (a) That part preliminary to the Law.
   (b) The Law.
   (c) The part after the Law.
It will thus be seen that it is the Sinaitic Covenant, revealing the Law, which gives unity to the Hebrew Scriptures, and so from this covenant is derived the name Old Testament (covenant).

3. *The Manner in which the Law is Recorded.*
   (1) In the order in which it was given.
   (2) Interspersed with history. It is not in a collected and digested form as the laws of a state, but like doctrine, it is mixed up with other things. From this fact it follows:
       (a) We must interpret the law in the light of the history.
       (b) Collate scattered portions of the law, here a part and there a part.

4. *Whence Given.* From Mt. Horeb until the tabernacle was set up. Ex. 19:9. The cloud seems to have stood upon the mount to show where Jehovah was, but when the tabernacle was set up God dwelt there. Ex. 40:34. The law was given from the bosom of the cloud, whether on Mt. Horeb or the tabernacle. Lev. 1:1.—*II.*

5. *The Order in which the Law was Given.*
   (1) The preparation for the divine revelation. Ex., chap. 19.
   (2) Giving of the Ten Commandments. Ex. 20: 1–17.
   (3) The general principles of the whole law. Ex. 20: 21 to chap. 24.

(4) Acceptance of the law by the people. Ex. chap. 24.
　(a) The covenant transaction. vs. 1–8.
　(b) The ratification of the covenant. vs. 9–11.
(5) The ritual. Especial law of the ritual. Ex., chaps. 25 to 31, inclusive. It opens with the tabernacle, and then gives direction how Aaron and his sons were to be consecrated to the priesthood.
(6) An important piece of history. The idolatry of the people and breach of the covenant by worship of the calves. This breach of the covenant symbolized by the broken stones. Ex., chaps. 32–33.
(7) Renewal of the covenant. Ex. 34.
(8) Actual building of the tabernacle and its consecration. Ex., chaps. 34–40.
(9) Whole law detailed and explained. Book of Leviticus.
(10) Various laws mingled with history and given under various circumstances as they arose and needed particular laws.
(11) General recapitulation of the law with a special relation to their use in Canaan.

1. The Sinaitic Covenant Described.

1. *The Mosaic Law Revealed in the Form of a Covenant.*
　(1) It is so styled. Deut. 5: 2; Heb. 8: 9; Jer. 31: 31.
　(2) The roll containing it is called the book of the covenant. Ex. 24: 7; 2 Kings 23: 2 and 21.
　(3) The tables of stone called the tables of the covenant. Deut. 9: 9, 11, 15.
2. *The Parties to it.* God and Israel. The generation of Israel who formally entered into this

covenant acted, not only for themselves, but also for the succeeding generations of their descendants, so that this covenant was really between God and all the generations of Israel up to the coming of Christ.

3. *The Covenant.* How given and received? God the giver, man the receiver. This a fundamental truth, and is the only constant and common thing in every covenant of God with man. God, as the infinite sovereign, gives, proposes. Man must receive or reject *as* God proposes, without making any counter propositions or changes. This feature of the covenant seen.

    (*a*) Before the covenant was given. Ex. 19:3-8.

    (*b*) After the covenant was given. Ex. 24:3.

    (*c*) In the covenant as written. Ex. 24:4-7. The difference between a law and a covenant is this: A law may be imposed without the consent of one party, while in a covenant there must be the consent of both parties. In this covenant the consent of the Jews was given three times.

4. *How Ratified.*

    (1) By a monumental altar. Ex. 24:4. Built where it was given, and around it twelve pillars for the twelve tribes—the altar representing God.

    (2) By sacrifice on the altar. Ex. 24:5-8; Heb. 9:19.

    (3) By a covenant feast. Ex. 24:9-10. God the host, and the elders his guests. In this ratification the germ of two things: ratifica-

tion by blood (crucifixion), and Lord's Supper.

5. *The Substance of the Covenant is the Law of God, not only the Moral, but the Ceremonial and Civil.* Ex. 24 : 4–10. Indeed, the whole Sinai transaction is the law reduced to the form of a covenant. Law is the subject-matter of the covenant.

6. *The Mutual Stipulations.*
   (1) On the part of God:
      (*a*) By way of promises. Ex. 19 : 3–8 ; 20 : 12 ; Deut. 11 : 13–32 ; 28 : 11–14.
      (*b*) By way of threats. Deut. 27 : 10–26 ; 28 : 15–68.
   (2) On the part of the people. Ex. 19 : 8 ; 24 : 3. This promise embraced the whole law—Moral, Ceremonial, Civil.

7. *Relation to Abrahamic Covenant.*
   (1) Both were intended to raise up an holy seed ; not a nation simply, but a church. See Ten Commandments, whole law of purifications. Lev. 20 : 25–26 ; 22 : 31–33.
   (2) Both intended to isolate the chosen seed. This idea the foundation of many laws. Ex. 34 : 10-10 ; Lev. 20 : 24–26.
   (3) Both exhibited Christ. The Abrahamic in promise, the Sinaitic in types, as seen in the whole sacrificial and sacerdotal system. Gal. 3 : 24–25. It was a great educational system to prepare the way for Christianity, styled pedagogic.
   (4) The Sinai Covenant was added to the Abrahamic because of transgressions. Gal. 3 : 19, *i. e.*, the Abrahamic covenant could not re-

strain men from sin, therefore the law, with its terrible sanctions and dreadful curse, was added to aid.

(5) The Sinai covenant was temporary, the Abrahamic permanent. Gal. 3 : 19. N. T. *passim.*

(6) Summarily stated thus: The Sinai covenant was in furtherance of and executive of the Abrahamic covenant. It fulfilled to the people the temporal blessings of the Abrahamic and opened up the way for the spiritual. It was a temporary institute to help along the permanent one, and to give it force.

8. *The Law Embraced in the Covenant.*
   (1) The Moral Law.
   (2) The Ceremonial Law.
   (3) The Civil Law.

II. The Moral Law or Decalogue. Ex. 20: 2-17; Deut. 5: 6-21.

1. *Its Importance.* (Dabney.)

(1) Indicated by manner in which it was given: spoken by Jehovah himself to his Church in an audible voice (Acts 7 : 53), with the terrible adjuncts of clouds, and thunders, and lightnings, and the sound of a trumpet. Ex. 19 : 16-25 ; 20 : 1.

(2) These *Ten Words* the only part of revelation thus spoken. Deut. 5 : 22.

(3) These ten precepts were then twice graven by God himself on tables of stone ; the imperishable material signifying the perpetuity of the laws ; and these tables were to be kept

among the most sacred things of their religion.

(4) Christ's summary of Man's duty into the two precepts of love to God and love to man evidently an abridgment of the Decalogue. He said that on these two abridged commands hang all the law and the prophets. Therefore, all the Old Testament hangs on the Decalogue, of which these two are the epitome.

2. *Divisions.* (See Dabney.)

(1) Into two tables—called tables from the fact that the Decalogue was written by God on two tables of stone. Expositors have been divided as to what commands belong to the first table or division, and which to the second. "It is now generally held that four precepts composed the first table, and six the second. This is the natural division. Of the duties enjoined in the first four, God is the direct object; of those inculcated in the last six, man is the direct object. Thus, we conform to our Saviour's summary: love to God and love to man."

(2) Into ten separate commands. (Repeat preface, then the Ten Commandments.)

3. *Convenient Analysis of Thos. Aquinas* (Humphrey).

The first table commands us to honor God (1) in His Being, (2) in His Worship, (3) in His Name, (4) in His Day of Rest, and (5) in His Representatives. The second table: Thou shalt not injure thy neighbor in (1) his life, (2) his family, (3) his property, (4) name, nor (5) in thought.

4. *The Grand Purposes of the Decalogue* (Humphrey). (1) To testify against sinners. Ex. 31:18; 32:15.
   (2) To furnish them with a rule of life, which rule they were required to obey.
   (3) To give to all men a knowledge of the law of God.
5. *Rules of Interpretation* (Dabney).
   (1) The law is spiritual. Rom. 7:14. Matt. 5: 21–22.
   (2) In each precept, the chief duty or sin is taken as representative of the various lesser duties or sins of that class; and the overt act is taken as the representative of all related affections and under it they are all enjoined or forbidden. Thus our Saviour teaches us that under the head of murder, angry thoughts and abusive words are also forbidden.
   (3) Commandment implied in prohibition. "To command a given class of duties plainly implies a prohibition of the opposite class of sins, and *vice versa.*"
   (4) The precepts of the first table containing duties to God are superior in obligation to the precepts of the second table containing duties to man. Luke 14:26.

III. Ceremonial Law.

INTRODUCTION.

1. *Typology of Scriptures.* (Humphrey.)
   (1) What relation does the Mosaic dispensation bear to the Christian?
      (*a*) That of the transient to the permanent.
      (*b*) Of the pedagogic to the final. Gal. 3: 17–24. It preceded it in point of time

and taught of the only living and true
God, and the principles of divine law.
It was a great scheme of religious education
to teach elementary truth. Two
cautions: (*aa*) The old dispensation
was divine and perfect to its ends. 2
Cor. 3 : 7–11. A glorious dispensation,
but only preliminary. (*bb*) Do not look
for too much in the Old Testament rendering
the New unnecessary, nor look for
too little rendering it obsolete and useless.

(2) What are the chief criteria of a type?

  (*a*) A real person or thing in the Old Testament
corresponding to a real person or
thing in New Testament—*e. g.*, Adam to
Christ. Rom. 5 : 12 ; 1 Cor. 15 : 45.
Sacrifice to Christ's atonement. The
reality rules out and distinguishes a type
from an allegory. An allegory is a fictitious
narrative illustrating some truth.
(In Gal. 4 : 22 " allegory " is used in its
popular sense.)

  (*b*) There must be a resemblance between
the type and antitype—*e. g.*, lifting up
serpent and Christ, manna and Christ.
John 3 :14 ; 1 Cor. 10 : 3–4.

  (*c*) There must be a divine appointment constituting
the person or thing a type. It
is a fundamental requisite that it be ordained
of God. Did God appoint it?
determines difference between type and
simile or illustration.

  (*d*) The type represents an object yet future.
Col. 2 : 17 and Heb. 10 : 1 show distinction
between type and symbol. The sym-

bol belongs to the present or very near future—*e. g.* 1 Sam. 7 : 12 ; 10: 1 ; Jer. 1 : 11–14 ; 13 : 1–11. A type is a prophetic symbol.

(3) What does the idea of the type presuppose?

   (*a*) That God from the beginning determined what should come to pass in the New Testament.

   (*b*) That he put things in a train to bring about these blessings.

   (*c*) That he put into the Old Testament persons or things as types foreshadowing what he resolved to do in the New Testament—*e. g.*, he resolved to send his son into the world; he put things in a train to bring it about, and so put in Old Testament types of his son.

(4) Relation of types to prophecy. The type prefigures and the prophecy foretells the good things to come. Their object the same, the manner different—one a picture, the other the printed book. The Priest in his robes a picture, the Prophet at his side the written book ; the one more beautiful and striking, the other more clear and distinct. The book explains the picture.

(5) How may we know what persons or things are typical? Two ways—one definite and satisfactory, the other indefinite and unsatisfactory.

   (*a*) Whatever in the Old Testament is declared in the New Testament to be a type is certainly a type—*e. g.*, Melchizedek. Gen. 14 : 18, cf. Heb. 7 ; Ezek. 37 : 24, cf. Luke 1 : 32 ; Sanctuary, Heb. 9.

(b) Whatever can be shown by fair exposition to be intended by God himself for a type is to be taken as such. Debatable ground.

(6) Hints as to the interpretation of types.

(a) Be not misled by fanciful analogies and resemblances, as oak of Absalom; Moses with outstretched arms representing the cross; skins of tabernacle dyed red the blood of the martyrs, etc.

(b) Adhere rigidly to the idea that nothing is a type unless divinely appointed for that end. Did God appoint them as types? This would rule out such suppositions as that the bells and pomegranates in the robes of the priest—the bells the glad tidings and the pomegranates the sweet fragrance of the gospel.

(c) In expounding Old Testament use the words *type* and *typify* with caution. If it is a divine ordinance you can call it a type, but not if it is only a *resemblance*. In the one case you are expressing the thought of God, and in the other your own.

(d) Do not push a type too far. The brazen serpent a type of Christ in only one or two points. See also Jonah, Matt. 12 : 30.

(7) How many classes of types? Two—Historical and Ritual. The first class comprises Historical persons and events, as Moses, David, Manna, etc. The second class embraces the ceremonies of the Ritual law.

2. *The Two Great Purposes of this Law.*
   (1) Intended primarily for the Hebrews, for their instruction and spiritual culture.
   (2) Prospective and to prepare the way for Christianity.
3. *Two Elements in the Ceremonial Law Corresponding to These Two Purposes. Symbols and Types.* Recall the meaning of these terms. A symbol is a sensible sign of an insensible reality—*e. g.*, elements in Lord's Supper; a type is a prophetic symbol. As far as this law was for the Jews immediately it was symbolical. So far as it was designed to foreshadow the gospel it was typical. Hence these institutions of Moses were both symbolical and typical.
4. *The Clew to the Interpretation of the Law Lies in these Questions:*
   (1) What is its symbolical meaning?
   (2) What is its typical meaning?
5. *Divisions of the Ceremonial Law.*
   (1) Sacred places, or the sanctuary.
   (2) Sacred persons, or the priesthood.
   (3) Sacred rites, or the ritual.
   (4) Sacred times, or the calendar.

First. The Sanctuary.
1. *Its Origin.* (See Hurlbut, p. 135.)
2. *History of its Erection.*
   (1) God raised up the architects by special call and inspiration. Ex. 31 : 1-6.
   (2) The materials were provided (*a*) By the atonement money. Ex. 30 : 11-16. (*b*) By the voluntary contributions of the people. Ex. 35 : 4-9, 20-29. Did they give enough? Ex. 36 : 4-6.

THIRD PERIOD. 119

(3) Their value. Ex. 38 : 24–30. Difficult to ascertain for two reasons:
  (a) We cannot exactly determine the value of the shekel or talent. In time of Christ the shekel was ½ oz. of silver, say 50 cents; in gold, $8.00; a talent was 3,-000 shekels; in silver, $1,500.00; in gold, $24,000.00.
  (b) The commercial value of gems, precious stones, embroidery, etc., cannot be determined. Probable value of all, $1,-200,000.00.
(4) Whence obtained? Gen. 15 : 14; Ex. 12 : 35.
(5) When was the tabernacle finished? One year after the Exodus (Ex. 40 : 17); nine months from the giving of the law. Ex. 19 : 1.

3. *Its Structure.*
  (1) Dimensions: Length, 30 cubits, 45 feet (Geikie); breadth, 10 cubits, 15 feet; height, 10 cubits, 15 feet. Holy of holies, 10 cubits each way: A perfect cube.
  (2) Its framework: Pillars, Ex. 26 : 32; bars, Ex. 26 : 26–29; planks, Ex. 26 : 15–25.
  (3) Its curtains or covering:
    (a) The inner curtain, linen, Ex. 26 : 1–6.
    (b) The second curtain, goat's hair, 26 : 7–13.
    (c) The third curtain, ram skins, 26 : 14.
    (d) The outer curtain, seal skins, 26 : 14.
  (4) The veils of the tabernacle:
    (a) Of the eastern entrance. 26 : 36.
    (b) Within. Ex. 26 : 31; Heb. 9 : 3.
  (5) Divisions of the tabernacle:
    (a) The court. Ex. 27 : 9–14. Of this, the eastern end and entrance were closed by hangings of costly workmanship, though

not of the same exceptional fineness as that of the inner curtains. It is supposed that the veil which hung around the court was of network, so that all the people could see the sacrifice. The dimensions of this enclosure were 100 cubits long and 50 cubits wide, about 150 feet by 75 feet.

 (*b*) The Holy place. This was the outer department of the tent, about 30 feet by 15 feet.

 (*c*) The Holy of Holies. This the inner department of the tent, 15 feet each way.

4. *The Furniture of the Tabernacle.*

 (1) In the Court two things, the brazen altar (Ex. 27: 1–8), and the laver (Ex. 30:. 17–21). The symbolical idea here is, " let no man go into the holy presence except after sacrifice and washing—*i. e.*, atonement and purification.

 (2) In the Holy place three things:

  (*a*) Altar of incense. Ex. 30: 1–10. Incense, how compounded. Ex. 30: 34–37.

  (*b*) The table of the shewbread. Ex. 25: 23–30; Lev. 24: 5–6.

  (*c*) Golden candlestick. Ex. 25: 31–40.

 (3) In Holy of Holies three things:

  (*a*) Ark of the covenant. Ex. 25: 10–16; 37: 1.

  (*b*) The mercy seat. A plate of gold laid on the ark as a covering. Ex. 25: 17.

  (*c*) The cherubim. Ex. 25: 18. Between them was the throne of God. The articles in the ark were the Law, Ex.

25 : 16; pot of manna, Ex. 16 : 33–34;
Aaron's rod, Num. 17 : 10, and Heb.
9 : 4. The Book of the Law was in the
side of the ark. Deut. 31 : 26.

5. *Its Dedication.*
   (1) Tabernacle finished. Ex. 40 : 20–33.
   (2) The Lord descending. Ex. 40 : 34.
   (3) The anointing. Lev. 8 : 10.
   (4) The descent of the holy fire. Lev. 9 : 24.
   (5) The offerings of the princes. Num. 7 : 10–88.
   (6) The holy oracle. Num. 7 : 89.

6. *Its After-History.*

   The Israelites carried it with them through the wilderness and into Canaan, where it was their only place of worship for five hundred years. When they crossed the Jordan, it was first set up in Gilgal, and after the conquest in Shiloh, where it remained about three hundred years. After the defeat of Israel by the Philistines (1 Sam. 4: 1–11), the tabernacle seems to have been removed to Nob, in the tribe of Benjamin, where it remained until Saul's slaughter of the priests. 1 Sam. 21 : 1–6 ; 22 : 18–19. It seems to have been at Gibeon while the ark was in seclusion at Kirjath-jearim. 2 Chr. 1 : 4 (Hurlbut). Finally it was superseded by the temple.

7. *Its General Significance.*
   (1) A tent for Jehovah. Ex. 25 : 8.
   (2) Made after a divine pattern. Ex. 26 : 30 ; Heb. 8 : 5 ; Ex. 39 : 43.

Reasons for this Minuteness.

    (*a*) That the people might be impressed with the authority of God in everything, even the most minute.

    (*b*) It was intended as a type of heavenly things; but the idea of a type involves divine appointment.

(3) It was exceedingly beautiful and costly. "For beauty and for glory."

(4) Intended for worship by a representative. It was a small building, yet the only place of worship for all the twelve tribes. Therefore worship was to be allowed by a few for many.

8. *The Encampment.* In the center was the tabernacle. Moses' and Aaron's tent in front (Num. 3: 38); the Levites around and next to the tabernacle; the tribes divided into four divisions and encamped in front, behind, and on either side.

9. *The March.*

  (1) Preparation. Num. 4: 5–16, 25–31.

  (2) Order of march. Num. 2: 9–31.

10. *Spiritual Uses, Threefold: Direct, Symbolical, and Typical.*

  (1) Direct uses—*five*.

    (*a*) The place of worship for the Hebrews. So far as we know it was the first structure ever erected for the worship of the true God. They had built altars before, but nothing in the way of a house.

    (*b*) A tent for Jehovah, King of Israel. Lev. 16: 2; Ps. 80: 1.

    (*c*) The place of the oracle. While at

THIRD PERIOD. 123

Sinai the cloud was on the mount. But afterwards on the tabernacle. Ex. 40 : 34 ; Lev. 1 : 1 ; Ex. 25 : 22.

 (d) The place of meeting of Jehovah with the people. The phrase, "tabernacle of the congregation," wherever used, should be translated "tent of meeting." See Revised Version. The word "meeting-house" is a place where God meets with his people, and not of people meeting together.

 (e) A place of deposit for the tables and book of the law. Deut. 31 : 26 ; Num. 17 : 7 ; Acts 7 : 44.

(2) Its symbolical uses.

 (a) The grand truth was: *That God had his dwelling-place among men.* He was in the *center* of the encampment, with the cloud over it as a token of his presence. Ex. 25 : 8 ; 29 : 45.

 (b) Approach to God can only be made through atonement and purification.

 (c) The mercy seat, placed above the tables of the law, signified a covering for sin. And inasmuch as the mercy seat was sprinkled with blood, it signified that the law was covered by the atonement. Mercy through atonement.

 (d) Altar of incense symbolical of prayer. Ps. 141 : 2 ; Rev. 5 : 8.

 (e) Candlestick symbolical of the diffusion of truth. Matt. 5 : 14 ; Rev. 1 : 20.

 (f) Shewbread symbolical of communion with God.

(3) Its typical meaning.
   (a) The inhabitation of Christ among men. Matt. 1:23; John 1:14; 2:19.
   (b) The most holy place typical of heaven. See Hebs.
   (c) For typology of furniture, see Heb., chap. 9.

Caution.—The symbolical and typical meaning of the tabernacle limited.
   (1) Seek no spiritual meaning in the minor details of the building.
   (2) Seek none in those things wherein the tabernacle differed from the temple—*e. g.*, acacia wood.
   (3) Seek none in each of the various ornaments or colors.
   (4) Be not misled by fanciful analogies. Follow sound judgment, and interpret it by other Scripture.

Second. Sacred Persons or the Priesthood.
1. *The Vocation of the Aaronic Priesthood.*
   (1) Aaron and his sons called of God. This call first given through Moses (Ex. 28:1); then to Aaron himself. Num. 18:1; Heb. 5:4.
   (2) This call afterwards indisputably vindicated. Num., chap. 16 (censers); Num., chap. 17 (Aaron's rod).
   (3) To be perpetuated by hereditary transmission in the Aaronic line. Did not fail for 1,500 years.
   (4) The Levites made assistants to Aaron and his sons. Num. 18:1–7.

2. *Qualifications for Office of Priest.*
   (1) Age. Not distinctly stated at what age the priest entered or left his office. Some draw inferences from the statements concerning the Levites. The age limits of those who carried the furniture in the march were from 30 to 50. Num. 4:23; of those who ministered in the tabernacle from 25 to 50. Num. 8:24-25. Again it was probably from 20 to 50. 1 Chr. 23-24. Law changed according to circumstances. See 2 Chr. 31:17; Ezra 3:8.
   (2) Freedom from bodily defect. Lev. 21:17-23.
   (3) Ceremonial holiness. Ex. 29:4, 10, 15, 19, etc.
3. *The Dress of the Sacerdotal Order.*
   (1) The dress of the high priest.
      (a) The Ephod. Ex. 28:6-14. "The Ephod was the distinctive priestly garment (see 1 Saml. 2:28). It hung upon the shoulders down to the waist, and was formed of the most costly and beautiful materials, corresponding exactly to those employed in the interior decoration of the Holy Place. The girdle was made of the same materials with the same combination of colors. . . . But the most important part of the Ephod was the shoulder pieces, on which were set two onyx stones, with the names of the tribes engraven on them—six on the one and six on the other." v. 12.—*Mosaic Era* (*Gibson*), p. 183.

(b) The Breastplate. vs. 15–30. On "this were set in gold twelve different precious stones; and on these again were engraven the names of the twelve children of Israel." (See v. 29.) "Not only on his shoulders, the seat of strength, but on his heart, the seat of love." "The Urim and Thummim (v. 30) which were 'to be put in the breast-plate,' are not described, and therefore we cannot tell with certainty what form the representation took. The words mean 'lights and perfection'; and, inasmuch as the idea of guidance is regularly associated with the Urim and Thummim," the idea seems to be—guidance from the Father of lights, and the glory (perfection) to which that light leads.—*Gibson*.

(c) The Robe of the Ephod (vs. 31-35). This was a long robe worn under the Ephod, and appearing below it. It was all of blue and had fringe, to which were attached pomegranates and bells. From this was derived the Romish idea of ringing little bells to give notice of priest's approach.

(d) The Mitre. vs. 36–38. This was a plate of pure gold, on which was inscribed, Holiness to the Lord. This plate, in a setting of blue, was to be worn upon the forehead.

(2) The dress of the priests. Ex. 28: 40–43.

4. *The Consecration of the Sacred Order.*

(1) Of Aaron and his sons. Ex. 29. The ceremony embraced the following things:

(a) Washing. v. 4. Signifying the necessity of ceremonial holiness in order to approach God.

(b) Investiture. vs. 5–9. "It was by the putting on of the appointed *garments* that Aaron and his sons were invested with office."

(c) Sacrifice. 10–15.

(d) Anointing. vs. 21 and 29; Lev. 8:12. "The meaning of the anointing is unmistakable, for throughout the Scriptures oil is the familiar and consistent symbol of divine grace; and as the Holy Spirit is the fountain of divine grace, the anointing is symbolical of his gracious work." —*Gibson*.

(e) The ram of consecration. vs. 15–37. Lev. 8:22–28.

(2) Of the Levites. Numb. 8:5–23.

5. *Functions of the Priestly Office.*

(1) The priest represented the people. This a fundamental idea. It was signified (a) By his dress. On his shoulders the onyx stones bearing the names of the twelve tribes. So also the Breastplate. Ex. 28:9–15. (b) By the law of sacrifice. He offered sacrifice, burnt offering, incense, etc., for them. Lev. 16.

(2) He was the sole officer of sacrifice. Numb. 3:10; 16:40; 18:3, 4, 7; Heb. 5:1.

(3) Mediator between God and man. Ex. 28:15–38.

(4) The religious teacher of the people. Lev. 10:11; Deut. 33:10. He did not teach them so much orally as pictorially.

(5) Bearer of the oracle—the Urim and Thummim. Little known. Probably indicated some official function of the High Priest.

6. *The Support of the Priesthood.*
   (1) Forty-eight cities scattered throughout all the tribes and surrounded by three hundred acres of land. Josh. 21; 1 Chr. 6:54–84.
   (2) The tithes. Numb. 18:20–24. These a tenth part of the *gross* proceeds. A tenth of the tithes assigned to the priests. Numb. 18:26–32.
   (3) The first fruits. Lev. 23:10; Numb. 18:12-13; Deut. 18:4.
   (4) The flesh of the first-born of animals. The fat was burned, and the blood sprinkled on the altar. Numb. 18:15–18. The first-born of man and of unclean beasts were to be redeemed. Numb. 18:15–16.
   (5) A share in the things offered. Lev. 6:25–26; 7:1–9; Ex. 29:26–29.

7. *The Symbolical Meaning of the Office.* Indicated to the people:
   (1) That they needed a divinely appointed mediator between God and them, for they could only come into God's presence and offer sacrifice *through the priest.*
   (2) That this mediator must be a representative man.

8. *Typical Meaning.* Very important. See Hebrews, which is an inspired commentary on it.
   (1) The Aaronic priesthood typified the divine vocation of Christ. Ex. 28:1 compared with Heb. 5:4.

(2) Typified the holiness of Christ. In the priest, ceremonial holiness; in Christ, essential holiness. Heb. 7 : 26.
(3) Typified the representative relation of Christ. Heb. 9 : 24; John 17 : 9.
(4) Typified the mediatorship of Christ. Lev. 16 : 40; Heb. 9 : 15.
(5) Typified his atonement for sin. Compare Lev. 4 : 20–35 and Heb. 9 : 11–15.
(6) Typified his intercession. Compare Lev. 16 : 15 with Heb. 9 : 24; 7 : 25.

Third. The Ritual or Sacred Rites and Ceremonies.

INTRODUCTORY.
1. *The Relation of the Ritual to the Ceremonial Law.* It is the central part of it. The sanctuary was constructed with reference to it. True also of the priesthood and calendar.
2. The rites may be distributed into two great classes—

A. SACRIFICES AND OFFERINGS.
B. PURIFICATIONS.

A. SACRIFICES AND OFFERINGS. Divided into two classes: 1. *The Bloody.* 2. *The Bloodless.*
1. *The Bloody Sacrifices and Offerings.* The kinds of animals offered. They were only the animals used for food, and of five kinds: (1) Ox kind, (2) sheep, (3) goats, (4) turtle dove, (5) pigeon. The reason for this choice was probably twofold: (1) To indicate that the wealth of the nation belonged to God. (2) Because the flesh was to be eaten at the altar as a part of the ceremony. The *place* of the sacrifice was, by express command, the great altar be-

fore the tabernacle. The minister of sacrifice, the priest only. Numb. 3:10; 16:40; 18:3-7.

The following are the different kinds of bloody sacrifices and offerings:

(1) The whole burnt offering. "It was so called because the whole body of the victim, the skin only excepted, which was the priest's perquisite (Lev. 7:8), was burned, Lev. 1:6-9. It was also styled Olah, ascension, because it went up to God in the smoke thereof. (Dr. Humphrey, Preparing to Teach, p. 86.) Characteristics of the Olah:

(a) The most ancient form of sacrifice. Lev. 1:3-9 and 6:9-13.

(b) The basis of the entire ritual: "The burning entered as an integral element into all the forms of the bloody offerings; into the sin, the trespass, and the peace offering. Blood and fire were invariably seen in every one of the expiatory rites."

(c) It was renewed twice daily from day to day, and was, therefore, a "continual burnt offering." The fire never went out, the smoke never ceased to ascend day or night. Ex. 29:42; Numb. 28:3-6.

(d) "This was the general comprehensive offering for sin as sin and for the sin of the race as a whole. Offerings for particular sins, whether of individuals or of all Israel, took the specific form of the sin, or trespass, or the peace offering. The Olah was in the nature of a general act of worship and expiation for sin, without special reference to the guilt of the individual, or even, of the Hebrews as the chosen people. 'Behold the Lamb of God, which taketh away the sin of the world.'"

(2) The sin offering. Lev. 4 to 5: 14.

  (a) "*Like* the Olah, it was expiatory. Blood was shed and sprinkled on the furniture of the sanctuary and was poured in floods over the altar of burnt offering in the fore-court."

  (b) "*Unlike* the Olah, it was expiatory of *particular* sins and the sins of *individuals*."

  (c) "*Unlike* the Olah, the fat only was burnt, and the kidneys, because these organs were imbedded in large deposits of fat. The flesh was otherwise disposed of. Lev. 4: 8, 10-15."

  (d) "The greater sin offering was presented (1) for the high priest when he was guilty of crime (Lev. 4: 3-12); (2) for a sin of the whole people (Lev. 4: 13-21); (3) on the great day of atonement (Lev. 16: 26)."

  (e) "The lesser sin offering was presented (*aa*) by the ruler (Lev. 4: 22-26); (*bb*) by the private person (Lev. 4: 27-35); (*cc*) in various purifications, 12: 6; 14: 19.

(3) The trespass offering: The full distinction between the sin, and the trespass offering has not, perhaps, been ascertained, but the following are points upon which they differ:

  (a) "The trespass offering was never presented for the guilt of the whole people. That was a peculiarity of the sin offering."

(b) "The trespass offering was presented when the idea of restitution for injuries done was introduced into the service. Lev. 6: 1–7. This offering belonged in a special sense, to trespass against human rights. Lev. 6: 1–6; 7: 1–7; Num. 5: 6–8."

(c) "It was an inferior form of the sin offering. This appears (aa) from the occasion on which it was offered, and (bb) the blood was not taken into the sanctuary, nor put on the horns of the altar of burnt offering, but was simply sprinkled round about on the altar. Lev. 5: 9; 7: 2."

(d) "Christ is said in 2 Corinthians 5: 21, to be made a sin offering for us; but nowhere is he called a trespass offering, for the reason that the notion of our making restitution for our sins as against God is excluded."

(4) Peace offering. Lev. 7: 11–21.

(a) "It was generally presented by way of thanksgiving for mercies received. 2 Saml. 15: 8; Ps. 66: 13–15."

(b) "Expiation for sin was an essential element in the ceremony, showing that thanksgiving to God could not be separated from confession for sin. This was one of the fatal defects in Cain's offering."

(c) "The *votive* and *free-will* and *thank* offering were the three forms of the peace offering. The wave and heave offering took their name from the ceremony of waving or heaving a portion of the victim, say the shoulder, toward the altar or the holy of holies. Hence the 'wave breast' or 'heave shoulder.' Lev. 7 : 32–34. The peace offering was then, in all its varieties, essentially *eucharistic.* Hence its social and festive character, by which it was distinguished from the sin offerings and trespass offerings."—*Barrow, Bib. Antiq., p.* 580. After all the ceremonies of the sacrifice had been completed, the priest and his friends feasted joyfully before the Lord on the remainder. Lev. 7 : 11, etc.

2. *The Bloodless Offerings* (*Oblations*), *called in our version Meat Offerings;* of two kinds:

(1) Supplementary to the sacrifices. Such were the cakes and wafers of unleavened bread connected with the peace offering at Aaron's consecration (Lev. chap. 8); and the oblations of fine flour mingled with oil and wine, that were always to accompany the burnt offerings and peace offerings. Numb. 15: 2–8. Such also was the salt which, according to the Jewish interpretation of Leviticus 2: 13, accompanied every sacrifice as well as oblation. Ez. 43:24 ; Mark 9 : 49.—*Barrow, Bib. Ant., p.* 581.

(2) Independent of sacrifices (*e. g.,* Lev. chap. 2). "The bloodless offerings were not expiatory, but rather expressions of love, gratitude and devotion to God on the part of the giver."— *Barrow.*

B. PURIFICATIONS.

"The distinctions of clean and unclean entered

very deeply into the life of the Hebrews, continually meeting them in their public, as well as in their private and social relations."—*Barrow*. The importance attached to these distinctions of clean and unclean and attendant rites of purification indicated by the space given to the subject in the Scriptures. Lev. chaps. 11–15 and Num. 19; besides frequent references elsewhere.

1. *The Distinctions between Clean and Unclean in Respect of Food.* Lev. 11. Why this distinction? Perhaps we cannot give all the reasons, but these seem apparent:
    (*a*) Promotive of physical purity and health undoubtedly true.
    (*b*) Educational. By familiarizing the people with this distinction in articles of food the idea was constantly kept before them of holy and unholy, clean and unclean, in the moral and spiritual sphere.
    (*c*) To keep the Jews separate from other nations.

2. *Uncleanness from Conditions of the Body.* Lev. chaps. 12–15. "The scriptural view of disease and all the weaknesses of man's mortal state is deep and fundamental. It traces them all to *sin* as their ultimate source. Not all maladies, however, produced ceremonial uncleanness. Here, also, as in the distinction of food, man's natural instincts were followed. All diseases that produced corruption in the body, or running sores, or a flow of blood, made the sufferer unclean; and the culmination of uncleanness was in death—(*a*) The curse denounced on man for sin, and the emblem chosen by the Holy

Ghost to represent the state of perdition into which sin brings the soul." Lev. 1:39–40; Num. 19:11–22. Leprosy, as a corruption of the living body, manifesting itself on its surface, and tending toward death, is an image of the corruption and death which sin brings to the soul; and is regarded in Scripture as emphatically the unclean disease.

3. *Restraints Laid on the Unclean.*
    (a) They were excluded from the privileges of the sanctuary. Lev. 15:31; Num. 19:13.
    (b) Lepers were shut out of the camp. Lev. 13:46; 14:17.

4. *The Process of Cleansing.* Varied in different cases, according to the nature of the defilement. In general embraced the following ceremonies:
  (1) Washing in water. Lev. 14:8; 15:13.
  (2) Cleansing by the use of ashes. See the ordinance of the red heifer in Num. 19; compare Heb. 9:13.
  (3) Hyssop and cedar were used to sweeten the unclean. Num. 19:6; Lev. 14:4.
  (4) A sacrifice, usually by the sin-offering. Lev. 14:10–32.
    "This fact is most important, showing that purification had direct reference to sin."—*Dr. Humphrey.*

5. *The Explanation of these Rites.* They were intended to set forth symbolically the defilement of sin and the necessity of purification. A twofold deliverance from sin necessary: (1) From the guilt of sin; symbolized in the ritual

by sacrifices and offerings (atonement). (2) From the defilement of sin; symbolized in the ritual by the ceremonies of purification.
6. *The Meaning of the Ritual.*
   (1) Symbolical meaning of the ritual. We must not look for symbols in every little detail. (See above on Typology.)
      (*a*) The imputation and transfer of sin from the offender to the animal. Lev. 4: 3, 4, 24; especially manifest in the laying of hands on the victim.
   (2) Remission of sin by shedding of blood. Lev. 17: 11; Heb. 9: 22.
   (3) The guilt (culpa) of sin requires atonement; symbolized in the sacrifices and offerings. The stain (macula) of sin requires purification; symbolized in the rites of purification. The rites, therefore, both expiatory and expurgatory.
7. *The Typical Meaning of the Ritual.*
      (*a*) The lamb typified Christ. John 1: 29.
      (*b*) The work of Christ in atoning for sin, and the work of the Spirit purifying from sin. See Heb.
      (*c*) Ritual, as a whole, typical of the gospel as a whole. Heb. chap. 9. "Shadow of good things to come."
8. *What was the Efficacy of the Mosaic Ritual?* How far did its atonements and purifications extend? Some say they were efficacious in some way or other to the believing worshipers. If so, what need of Christ and the Spirit? Others say it was an effete system. What need, then, of a divine revelation? The true answer lies between these two extremes, viz.:

(1) They did *not* work pardon of sin. Heb. 10: 4; Isa. 40: 16.
(2) These Levitical purifications did *not* inwardly renew the soul. Heb. 10: 13–14.
(3) These ordinances *did* restore to church privileges—*e. g.*, leper.
(4) These atonements did expiate certain civil offences. Lev. 4: 2–7. High crimes, such as idolatry, etc., could not be thus expiated.
(5) Their efficacy as to sin, considered as against God, was merely typical; pointing to the true atonement and purification. The analogy is the sacraments, which are signs of the blood of Christ and the washing of the Spirit. Hence the answer is: As far as the sin was against the ceremonial law, there was actual atonement; so far as sin was against God, there was typical atonement.

Fourth. The Calendar.

INTRODUCTION.

1. *The Importance of the Calendar.*
If there had been no divinely appointed times for the observance of the ritual, it would not have been observed—*e. g.*, the Sabbath and Christianity.
2. *The Distribution of Sacred Times.* Follows the rule of sevens.
    (1) The seven days, closing with the Sabbath.
    (2) The seven weeks, beginning with the Passover and closing with Pentecost.
    (3) The seven months, culminating in the month of feasts.
    (4) The seven years, closing with the Sabbatical year.

(5) The seven weeks of years, followed by Jubilee.—*Gibson.*

3. *The Relation of the Sabbath to the Calendar.* It was the basis of the whole system of sacred times. As the altar was the basis of the sanctuary, and the olah of the ritual, so the Sabbath of the calendar. All these were historical.

➤ 1. *The Sabbath.* The seven days closing with the Sabbath. The Sabbath had a threefold historical relation:

  (1) To the human race. Given to the race at creation. Gen. 2:2 ; Mark 2 : 27.

  (2) To Israel.

   (*a*) It was made a sign of the covenant between God and Israel. Ex. 31: 13. This did not abrogate the original meaning of the Sabbath, but gave it additional significance.

   (*b*) The violation of it was a capital crime. Ex. 31 : 14. All labor strictly forbidden. Numb. 15 : 35.

   (*c*) The worship on the Sabbath was distinguished by offering two lambs on the altar instead of one. Numb. 28 : 9 ; also the renewal of the shewbread. Lev. 24 : 5-9 ; cf. Matt. 12 : 5.

   (*d*) Symbolical of God's work in creation and deliverance from Egypt.

   (*e*) Typical of rest in promised land and in heaven. Heb. 4 : 4-8. Obs.—The ideas connected with the Sabbath as given to the Jews were, (1) Rest, Ex. 31 : 15 ; (2) Refreshment, Ex. 23 : 12 ; (3) Holiness, Ex. 31 : 14 ; (4) Joy, Isa. 58 : 13.

How untrue, then, that the Jewish Sabbath was a dreary bondage. "Not only so, but the entire Jewish system is often represented as dull, dreary and dolorous. On the contrary, it was characterized especially by times of feasting and rejoicing."—*Gibson*.

(3) Relation to Christianity.
   (*a*) It commemorates the resurrection of Christ.
   (*b*) This rendered another change necessary —a change of day. The philosophy of it is that as covenants were made it was adapted to each one. Looked at in this view, all difficulty vanishes.

2. *The Seven Weeks, beginning with the Passover and closing with Pentecost.* "This cycle of weeks was of yearly occurrence." The following was the order observed in this cycle:

(1) The Passover. This the beginning of the sacred year. Ex. 12:2. The feast of the Passover was, in the first place, commemorative. It celebrated the great deliverance from Egyptian bondage. But inasmuch as that deliverance was itself typical of the great salvation from sin, the ceremonial of the passover feast was typical of the means by which this great salvation was to be effected. 1 Cor. 5:7-8. The Passover feast occupied a day.

(2) "The feast of the Passover was immediately followed by the feast of 'Unleavened Bread,' lasting a week." Deut. 16:3-4; 1 Cor. 5:7-8. There was one day in the week of the feast which was specially signalized. It

was the day following the Sabbath of that week (Lev. 23 : 11). "On that day the first sheaf of the early harvest, the barley harvest, which at that season of the year was beginning to be gathered, was presented by waving to the Lord." Hence called Wave-sheaf-day. It occurred some time between March 25th and middle of April.—*Humphrey.*

(3) Pentecost. This was the day after the seven weeks closed. Lev. 23 : 15–16. "It marked the latter harvest. By this time the wheat harvest had been gathered in, and in accordance with this the characteristic ceremony of the day was the presentation by waving to the Lord of two loaves, baked from the meal of the recent harvest." Lev. 23 : 17. Pentecost also probably had a historical basis—the fiftieth day being the anniversary of the Lord's appearing on Sinai.

3. *The Seven Months, Culminating in the Month of Feasts.* "The month of the Passover was, as we have seen, the first month of the sacred year. The feast of Pentecost, coming as it did at the close of the seven-week cycle, occurred in the third month. But the culmination and crown of the sacred year was in the seventh month." Lev. 23:23–44.—*Mosaic Era, p.* 226. "There were three great occasions in this month," as follows:

(1) The Feast of Trumpets. vs. 23–25. The blowing of the trumpets summoned the people to a holy convocation, which ushered in the special joy of the specially sacred month. Num. 29 : 1–6; Ps. 81 : 3.

(2) The Great Day of Atonement. This occurred on the tenth day of the month. This was by far the most solemn and imposing of all the ceremonial observances. It is described at length in the sixteenth chapter of Leviticus.

(a) It was a day of fasting and sorrow and humiliation for sin. Lev. 23 : 27–29; 16 : 29–31.

(b) The day occurred very near the close of the civil year in October. Lev. 16 : 29. The sins of the people had been typically atoned for by the daily sacrifice and the continual burnt offering. But now the sins of the whole year were recapitulated, and a broad atonement was made for the accumulated mass of transgressions.

(c) The atonement was most thorough. The high priest made an atonement for himself and his family; for the people; for the holy place; for the most holy place; for the altar of sacrifice itself. vs. 6–20. See the summing up in verse 33.

(d) The services of the day summed up and recapitulated the entire ritual. All the animals used in daily sacrifice were now slain. vs. 3 5; the three great forms of sacrifice were used—the olah (v. 24), the sin offering (v. 25), and the burning without the camp (v. 27); all parts of the sanctuary and all its furniture were brought into use, the fore-court (v. 24), the holy place (v. 20), and the holy of holies (v. 14). The whole ritual system was reproduced. It was all there. The sanctuary in all its departments was entered. The priesthood was there in its highest representative. The ritual was there in the blood of bullock, ram and goat—this blood sprinkled everywhere; the burnt offering on the altar, the sin offering, the burning without the camp, were seen there. The day itself was a Sabbath of rest and affliction. Lev. 23: 32. The ceremonies made up an atonement for sin—for all sin—of all the people, an atonement for the altar and the sanctuary, and the mercy seat, unclean by the transgression of Israel.

(e) Ceremonies peculiar to this day. One of these was the entrance into the most holy place by the high priest. On this one day in the year only might the high priest go behind the veil. He went in during the day once with incense and blood for his own sins, and once with blood for the sins of the people. Lev. 16; Heb. 9:7-25. Another ceremony was that of the slain and the scapegoats. Lev. 16:7-10, 21-26. The symbolical meaning of this rite is plain. The atonement for sin includes two ideas, substitution for sin and its removal from the offender. Substitution was set forth by the goat slain at the door of the tabernacle. Its removal was represented by the acts of the high priest confessing over the other goat the iniquities of the people, putting them on its head, and sending it into the wilderness to return no more. Substitution for the sinner and the removal of his sin made up expiation. The slain goat was a symbol of the sin-sacrifice—the scapegoat of the sin-bearer. Still another of the ceremonies peculiar to this day was the burning of the victim without the camp. Heb. 13:11.—*Dr. Humphrey in Preparing to Preach, pp. 95-97.*

(3) The Feast of Tabernacles. "The great Day of Atonement was followed by a four days' pause, to give its solemn impressions time to be graven deeply on the people's souls, and then, on the fifteenth day of the month, the nation was summoned to the festivities and rejoicings of the great Feast of Tabernacles. Lev. 23:33-44."—*Gibson.*

Characteristics.

(*a*) Lasted seven days.

(*b*) "Commemorated the time when after leaving Egypt behind them the children of Israel gathered in their first camp of freedom at Succoth, where they had built themselves booths or leafy huts, whence the name."

(*c*) "Like the other great feasts, this also was associated with the labors of the husbandman. It was the great harvest festival, the harvest home of Israel. The entire product and vintage of the year were by this time gathered in, and accordingly it was known frequently as the Feast of Ingathering."

(*d*) It was marked by great rejoicing. "The sacred joy increased from day to day until the last day—that great day of the feast; concerning which it was a common saying of the Rabbis that he who had not seen the rejoicing of the people at that glad time had yet to learn what true joy was."

4. *The Seven Years Closing with the Sabbatical Year.* "Just as the last of every seven days was a Sabbath day, so the last of every seven years was a Sabbath year, according to the law in Leviticus. 25:1–7."—*Gibson.*

Two Leading Designs in the Sabbatical Year:
(1) "It is a year of rest *unto the land.*" v. 5.
(2) A severe test of their faith. How?

5. *The Seven Weeks of Years followed by Jubilee.* "The characteristic features of the Jubilee year, in addition to what it had in common with the Sabbatical year, are set forth in Lev. 25:10," and are as follows:
(1) "Ye shall hallow the fiftieth year."
(2) "Proclaim liberty throughout all the land unto all the inhabitants thereof."
(3) "Ye shall return every man unto his possessions, and ye shall return every man to his family."
(4) "It shall be a jubilee unto you."

IV. The Civil Law. (H.)

1. *The Fundamental Idea in the Structure of the Government was this: It was a Theocracy.* Ex. 19:4–9. God was their King and Ruler, as well as their God. He was as truly their King as Napoleon was King of France, and the tabernacle was his palace. The more perfectly this is comprehended, the clearer will be the view of the system.

(1) The outworking of this fundamental idea in legislation:
- (a) There was no power on earth to make new laws. Moses, Aaron, and all the people could neither make nor amend a single law; God was sole ruler, and all the lawmaking power was vested in him. See Num. 16.
- (b) It explains the minuteness of the Mosaic legislation. Lev. 19:19–27; Ex. 23:19. Minute legislation necessary to the prosperity of a nation, and God being the sole lawmaker, it was necessary he should give all laws needful for the nation's good.
- (c) It explains why war and peace were always declared by Jehovah, and not by the people. Daniel 1:41; Josh. 10:40; 1 Kings 12:24.

(2) Its outworkings as to crime:
- (a) It set aside the distinction between sin and crime, as we have it. With us, sin is against God, crime against the State; but there God was the State, and crime was sin.
- (b) Idolatry and kindred crimes were punished with death. The worship of other gods was treason. It was contempt of and rebellion against not only God, but also the actual sovereign of the State.
- (c) There was no power of pardon on earth when convicted of a capital crime; punishment was therefore certain. Pardon is always the act of a sovereign, and as God was the sovereign, no power on

earth could pardon. Heb. 10: 28; Num. 15: 30; Daniel 13: 6-10.

(3) It explains the position of the Kings of Israel. They were mere *viceroys*—theocratic kings— not supreme, but subordinate to God, the supreme sovereign. [Very important.]

2. *The Agrarian Law.* Agriculture was the leading pursuit of the people. Hence the importance of laws pertaining to land.

(1) The division of the country, (*a*) to the tribes, (*b*) to the families, (*c*) among the males of the family. Num. 26: 53; 33: 54.

(2) The land law connected with the Year of Jubilee. Lev. 25. Thus the inheritance of the family was preserved. An Israelite servant was freed in the Year of Jubilee and went to his farm. Lev. 25: 10. The object was to preserve it as an agricultural country, and keep it free from commerce.

(3) Daughters inheriting land must marry in their own family, in order that the land should not pass out of the family. Num. 27: 1-7; 36: 1-12.

3. *The Fundamental Principle in the Internal Organization of the People as a Nation was Tribal Independence with National Unity.* The United States form of government modeled after this.

(1) Tribal independence secured, (*a*) by the division of the country into tribal districts; (*b*) by the agrarian law preventing a man in one tribe from inheriting land in another; (*c*) by independent action in tribal affairs. Judges 1: 27-33.

(2) National unity secured, (*a*) by having only one high priest, one sanctuary, atonement, and

purification ; (b) by scattering the tribe of Levi throughout the whole nation (Num. 35) as lawyers, teachers, and physicians; (c) by the three great feasts of convocation assembling all the people together at the tabernacle ; (d) by a general convocation of the princes. Judges 20; 2 Sam. 3:17 ; 5:1.

4. *Laws for the Segregation of the Jews.*
   (1) Agrarian laws. (a) Encouraged agriculture. (b) Prevented foreigners from settling in the country. (c) Kept them from falling into the nomadic habits of those around them.
   (2) Marriage with the heathen forbidden. Deut. 7 : 3–4.
   (3) Their religious rites. Different from those of the heathen.
   (4) Various minute regulations putting a difference between the Jews and the heathen. Lev. 19:27; Ex. 23:19 ; Lev. 20:23; Acts 10 : 28.

5. *What are the Characteristics of the Penal Code?*
   (1) Number of capital crimes comparatively small — about twenty. A great contrast between them and the surrounding nations.
   (2) The trial was open and fair, in contrast with the secret tribunals of that time. At the gate of the city, Deut. 21:19; 25:6–7. Two witnesses necessary to convict, Num. 35:30 ; Deut. 17:6. Commanded not to receive bribes nor to do injustice to the poor, Ex. 23:8; Lev. 19:15. Witnesses confronted with the accused, Deut. 17:1–15.
   (3) Punishment not barbarous. When by whipping, not more than forty stripes. When

death, it was by stoning or hanging—chiefly the former. Sometimes by burning, Lev. 21:9. But it is supposed by all the Jews and most Christians that the burning was *post mortem*. They were first stoned, and then their bodies burned as an indignity.

(4) The family of the accused were not involved in his punishment, as in other nations, Deut. 24:16; cf. Dan. 6:24.

(5) Excision from the people, like excommunication from the church, and driving out of the camp sometimes included the idea of death.

(6) The cities of refuge for men committing excusable homicide. Num. 35:9–34; Josh. 20:7.

6. *Humane Provisions of the Law.*

(1) For the poor. Ex. 22:21–27; Lev. 19:9–10; Deut. 24:19.

(2) Care for the blind and deaf. Lev. 19:14.

(3) Servants. Lev. 25:39; Ex. 21:26.

(4) Law of the pledge. Deut. 24:10–14.

(5) As to beasts and birds. Ex. 20:10; Deut. 25:4; 22:6–7. All this breathes the spirit of the gospel—charity to all creatures, man, beast, birds—all made by God, and under his care.

SECTION 7. OTHER EVENTS AT SINAI.

NOTES.

1. *The Golden Calf.*
    (1) The scene in the camp. Ex. 32:1–6.
    (2) Scene on the mount. vs. 7–14.

death, it was by stoning or hanging—chiefly the former. Sometimes by burning, Lev. 21:9. But it is supposed by all the Jews and most Christians that the burning was *post mortem*. They were first stoned, and then their bodies burned as an indignity.

(4) The family of the accused were not involved in his punishment, as in other nations, Deut. 24:16; cf. Dan. 6:24.

(5) Excision from the people, like excommunication from the church, and driving out of the camp sometimes included the idea of death.

(6) The cities of refuge for men committing excusable homicide. Num. 35:9–34; Josh. 20:7.

6. *Humane Provisions of the Law.*

(1) For the poor. Ex. 22:21–27; Lev. 19:9–10; Deut. 24:19.

(2) Care for the blind and deaf. Lev. 19:14.

(3) Servants. Lev. 25:39; Ex. 21:26.

(4) Law of the pledge. Deut. 24:10–14.

(5) As to beasts and birds. Ex. 20:10; Deut. 25:4; 22:6–7. All this breathes the spirit of the gospel—charity to all creatures, man, beast, birds—all made by God, and under his care.

SECTION 7. OTHER EVENTS AT SINAI.

NOTES.

1. *The Golden Calf.*
   (1) The scene in the camp. Ex. 32:1–6.
   (2) Scene on the mount. vs. 7–14.

THE SINAITIC COVENANT.

The Covenant Described.

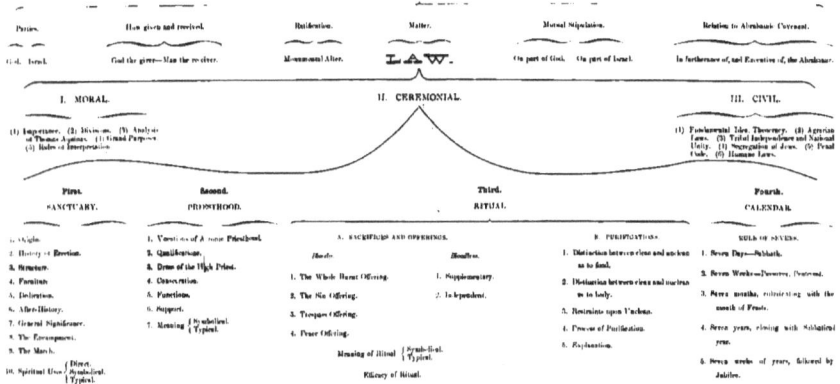

RULE OF SEVENS.

clean 1. Seven Days—Sabbath.

THIRD PERIOD. 149

(3) Moses' descent to the camp. vs. 15-35; 33 : 1-3.
(4) Effect upon the people. 33 : 4-6.
2. *Removal of the Tabernacle.* Ex. 33 : 7-10.
3. *God's Wonderful Interview with Moses.* 11-23.
4. *The Tables Renewed.* Ex., chap. 34.
5. *Nadab and Abihu Slain.* Lev. 10 : 1-7.
6. *The Blasphemers Stoned.* Lev. 24 : 10-16.
7. *The Census Taken.* Num., chap. 1.
8. *The Silver Trumpets.* Num. 10 : 1-10.

SECTION 8. FROM SINAI TO DEATH OF MOSES.

OUTLINE.

(Introduction.)
Hurlbut's Manual of Biblical Geography, p. 46.

I. From Sinai to Kadesh-Barnea.
Butler's Bible Work, (Numbers.)

II. Kadesh-Barnea.
Butler's Bible Work.
Geikie, Hours, chap. 11.

III. From Kadesh to Arnon.
Same references.

IV. Conquests East of the Jordan.
Humphrey, Ms. Notes of Lects.
Syllabus of O. T. Hist. Price.
Geikie, Hours, chap. 12.
Butler's Bible Work.
Hurlbut's Manual Bib. Geog., p. 51.

V. Deuteronomy.

Gibson, Mosaic Era, pp. 315–326.
Butler's Bible Work.

NOTES.

Introduction.

(1) The time of departure. Num. 10:11.
(2) The signal for the departure.
(3) The route. See Hurlbut, p. 46.
(4) Stations. Num. 33:16–49. See Hurlbut, pp. 47–48.

I. From Sinai to Kadesh-Barnea.

1. *The Order of March.* Num. 10:13–28.
2. *Hobab.* vs. 29–32.
3. *Taberah.* 11:1–3.
4. *Kibroth-hattaavah.* vs. 4–10, and 30–34.
5. *The Appointment of Elders.* vs. 11–29 (exp.).
6. *Miriam and Aaron against Moses.* Chap. 12. Why? What? Moses? The Lord? Miriam? Aaron? Moses?

II. Kadesh-Barnea.

"The location of this place is the great difficulty in the geography of the period. The name appears to be used with reference to a region, and more definitely referring to a place. Three localities have been claimed, all on the border of the 'Mount of the Amorites,' in the South Country." See Hurlbut, p. 47.

1. *The Spies.* Sent, 13:1–20; return, v. 25; reports, 26–33.
2. *Effect upon the People.* 14:1–4.
3. *Vain Efforts to Quiet Them.* vs. 5–10.
4. *The Provocation.* Cf. Heb. 3:8–11.

(a) Nature and cause of the provocation. 14 : 11 ; Heb. 3 : 18–19.
(b) God's threatening. v. 12.
(c) Moses' intercession. 13–19. Analyze.
(d) The judgment of God. Delivered first to Moses in answer to his prayer. 20–24; then to Moses and Aaron. vs. 26–35; then by Moses to the people. v. 39.
(e) The fate of the spies. vs. 36–38.
(f) Effect upon the people. vs. 40–45.

III. From Kadesh to River Arnon.

Time—about 38 years.

Sources of information. Num. chaps. 15 to 21 : 13; about five and a half chapters.

PRINCIPAL EVENTS.

1. *Rebellion of Korah.* Num. 16.

   (a) Parties were three, viz.: First, certain Levites, descendants of Kohath, jealous of the branch of the family to which Moses and Aaron belonged; second, certain descendants of Rueben (not reconciled to Reuben, being turned out of the birthright); third, certain chiefs of the other tribes—250 in number, who were unwilling to yield the functions of the priesthood which belonged to them before the law. Cf. Ex. 19 : 6 with Num. 16 : 2, and in the phrase "Kingdom of Priests" you have the root of this dangerous and formidable conspiracy.

   (b) It was a daring insurrection against God's authority. Everything was staked on crushing it, for if the scheme had succeeded God's whole plan would have failed.

(c) God met the emergency by the destruction of the company in a signal and open manner, before the whole camp. Num. 16 : 6–35.

(d) The memorials of the event. First, the brazen plate of the altar, 16 : 38 ; second, the budding of Aaron's rod. Chap. 17.

(e) The severity of God in the instance of Korah indispensable at this juncture. The subsequent event shows the alarming extent to which the spirit of rebellion had affected the whole congregation. vs. 41–50.

2. *The Death of Miriam.* 20 : 1.
3. *Sin of Moses and Aaron.* 20 : 2–13.
4. *Refusal of Edom.* vs. 14–21. Edom?
5. *Death of Aaron.* 20 : 22–29.
6. *The Destruction of Arad, the Canaanite.* 21 : 1–3.
7. *The Fiery Serpents.* 21 : 4–9 ; 2 Kings 18 : 4 ; John 3 : 14–15.

IV. Conquests East of the Jordan.

1. *Victory Over Sihon, King of the Amorites.* Num. 21 : 21–31.
2. *Victory Over Og, etc.* 21 : 32–35 ; Deut. 3 : 11 ; 31 : 4.
3. *The Story of Balaam.*

(a) The alliance between Moab and Midian. Num. 22 : 1–4.

(b) Balak sends for Balaam. Balaam was a magician living on the Euphrates. v. 5. "He was an Aramean by birth, and came from the region where the descendants

of Abraham still cherished, more or less
purely, the faith of the patriach; so that
he had learned to know Jehovah from
his own people."—*Geikie, Hours, p.* 201.
Balak probably had two objects in view
in sending for Balaam: one was he
thought the Israelites would wither under
his curse; another was it would encour-
age their soldiers.—*H.*

(c) Balaam's reply to first messengers, Num.
22:8-14; to second messengers. vs.
15-21. Rebuked in the way. vs. 22-35.

(d) Balaam's Four Prophecies:

First—Bamoth-baal. Num. 21:19-20; 22:41;
23:1-12. Altars; offerings; parable; points in
the parable.

(1) God has not cursed or defied Israel. v. 8.
(2) A peculiar people. v. 9.
(3) An innumerable people. v. 10.
(4) A reflection. v. 10.

Second—Pisgah, 23:13-27. Points in second
parable.

(1) God unchangeable. v. 19.
(2) This God has blessed Israel. v. 20.
(3) God is with Israel. v. 21.
(4) God has brought him triumphantly out of
Egypt. vs. 22-23.
(5) Israel shall be as a lion when he taketh his
prey. v. 24.

Third—Peor, 23:28-30; 24:1-14. Points in this
parable.

(1) Great prosperity and strength of Israel.
vs. 5-7.
(2) God the author of all this. vs. 8-9.

(3) God has, as it were, made common cause with Israel. v. 9.

Fourth Parable—Points.
(1) Messianic Prophecy. vs. 17–19.
(2) Destruction of Amalek. v. 20.
(3) Destruction of Kenites. vs. 21–22.
(4) Destruction of Asshur. v. 24.

We have here the case of a very bad man (Num. 25:1–5; 31:13–16; 2 Pet. 2:14–15; Rev. 2:14) who had the prophetic gift. How is this problem to be solved? Answer: Such is the law of God's dealing with man that he is pleased to bestow great gifts on wicked men, as on Judas Iscariot was conferred the power of working miracles. Mk. 3:14, etc. God makes use of men as instruments of his power who are not recipients of his grace. See the distinction between gifts and grace.—*H.*

V. Deuteronomy.

Introduction. "The name of the book is misleading if it conveys the impression, as it does to some, that it is only a repetition of what has gone before. In substance indeed it is the same, with some alterations and modifications, called for by the altered circumstances; but its form and purposes are quite different. The relation between the two may be illustrated by the difference between a report and the speech of the mover of it. Both productions have the same substance; the report records and the speech illustrates the same facts; yet the two may be, and ought to be, quite different. Moses, the author of this book. It is the eleventh month of the fortieth year. It is the eleventh hour of the Mosaic Era. The great law-giver and leader is about to be 'gathered to his fathers'; yet, 'his eye is not dim, nor his natural force abated.'" We are now to study his last words.

ANALYSIS.

1. *The Preface.* Author. v. 1. Place. vs. 1 and 5. Time. v. 3.
2. *The Three Addresses*—
   (*a*) First address. Chap. 1:5 to chap. 4, inclusive. General character, Historical, a review of the wanderings. Analyze.
   (*b*) The second address. Chaps. 5 to 26, inclusive. "As the first is based on the history and experience of the people, this one is founded on the Law, and therefore it may be considered as the Deuteronomy proper." Contains a *rehearsal; exposition* and *application* of the Law, together with such amendments as fitted it for Israel in a settled state. Notice prominence given to ten commandments. 5: 1–20.
   (*c*) The third address. Chaps. 27–30. As the first address was founded upon History, and the second upon Law, so the third was based upon the Covenant Transaction which followed the giving of the Decalogue with the statutes and judgments. "As the first law had been followed by a solemn ratification of the covenant where the altar and the twelve pillars were erected at the base of Sinai, so Moses gave directions for a still more solemn ratification when they should come into the land. 29: 1.

3. *Joshua Set Apart and Charged as Moses' Successor.* chap. 31.
4. *Moses' Dying Song.* chap. 32. Dr. Gibson, Mosaic Era, p. 326.

ANALYSIS.

Subject of the song: Jehovah and his People. Substance of it. vs. 3–6.
I. What Israel owed to God. 7–14.
II. How will Israel pay the debt? Sad prophetic picture. vs. 15–18.
III. How will God requite Israel? vs. 19–43.

5. *Moses' Blessings upon the Tribes.* chap. 33. This chapter "preserves the blessing wherewith Moses, the man of God, blessed the children of Israel before his death. Like the dying song, it is rich in poetry and full of majesty." Note specially vs. 26–29. "These words may be regarded as the crown of the Mosaic theology."—*Gibson.*
6. *Appendix.* chap. 34. View of the promised land. Death. Character.

SECTION 9. THE CONQUEST OF CANAAN.

OUTLINE.

(Introduction.)

Hurlbut, Manual of Bib. Geog., p. 51.
Humphrey, Manuscript Notes of Lects.
Butler's Bible Work.
Price, Syllabus of O. T. Hist.
Blaikie, Manual, chap. 7.
Barrow, Companion to Bible, p. 241.
Geikie, Hours, chap. 13.

I. **Preparatory to the Conquest.**
Same references.

II. **The Conquest.**
Same references.

III. **Partition of the Land.**
Hurlbut, Manual, etc., p. 55. Other references same as above.

IV. **Old Age and Death of Joshua.**
Humphrey, Ms. Notes of Lects.
Butler's Bible Work.
Geikie, O. T. Characters—Joshua.

V. **Supplementary to the Conquest.**
Hurlbut, Manual.
Price, Syllabus O. T. Hist.
Geikie, Hours, chap. 13.
Butler's Bible Work, Sec. 220.

VI. **The Extirpation of the Canaanites.**
Humphrey, Ms. Notes of Lects.
Butler's Bible Work, Sec. 208.

NOTES.

Introduction.

1. *Canaan* (*Western Palestine*).
    (1) Extent. From Dan to Beersheba is no more than 140 miles, and from the Mediterranean to Jordan the average breadth is only 40 miles, containing less than 6,000 square miles.
    (2) Physical features. The natural divisions of Canaan are three, the Coast Plain, the Mountain Region, and the Jordan Valley.
    (3) The inhabitants before the conquest. "When the Israelites, under Joshua, first entered the Promised Land, they found it in the possession

of a variety of races, in various stages of culture and civilization, and often engaged in war with each other. In the plains were the cities of the dissolute and effeminate Canaanites, on the sea-coast lived wealthy communities of merchants and sailors, while the mountain fastnesses were held by warlike clans whose ruined strongholds were the Ais, or 'stone heaps' of later times. The population was broadly distinguished into Canaanites, the inhabitants of the Canaan, or 'lowlands,' and Amorites, or Highlanders. . . . . Side by side with the names Canaanite and Amorite were two other names, which similarly had a descriptive rather than a national signification. These were Perizzite, or 'peasant,' and Hivite, or villager. . . Horite was another descriptive term of the same kind—the inhabitants of the caves with which the cliffs of Mount Seir were pierced. Equally descriptive, though in a different way, was the name of the Rephaim, or giants. . . . . The most prosperous and advanced of all the populations whom the Israelites found in Palestine were the Phœnicians on the coast."— *Butler's Bible Work*, Sec. 214.

(4) Adaptation of the land for its divine purpose and use.

    (*a*) Its physical character—soil, climate, etc.

    (*b*) Its isolation.

    (*c*) In the midst of the greatest and most cultivated nations of the Old World. "Altogether, it was impossible to conceive a region more wisely selected and in itself more thoroughly adapted for the purposes on account of which the family of Abraham was to be set apart."—*Butler's Bible Work.*

2. *Joshua.*
   (1) His intimate association with Moses. Ex. 17 : 9–16. "Whether Joshua was attached to Moses before this eventful day as his personal attendant, is not told us; but from this time he always appears in this character, as if brought into constant and confidential intercourse with the Head of the people, that he might be able hereafter to succeed him as its Leader. Henceforth his prospective dignity was foreshadowed by a change of name. Till the great day of the battle with Amalek he had been only Hosea—'Deliverance' or 'Salvation'; henceforth he should be Joshua or Jehoshua—The Salvation or Deliverance of Jehovah."—*Geikie.*
   (2) One of the spies. Numb. 13 : 8–16 ; 14 :6–9.
   (3) Joshua's appointment as Moses' successor. Deut. 31 : 1–23.
   (4) Formally inducted into office after death of Moses by Jehovah. Josh. 1 : 1–6.

3. *The Book of Joshua.* So called either because he wrote it or because he is the most prominent character in it.
   (1) Date of writing. Probably soon after the partition of Canaan. See Josh. 6 : 25 ; 14 : 5, 6, 14.
   (2) Author. Probably Joshua, though not certain. The Rabbis have a tradition to this effect (cf. Josh. 24 : 26). Last chapter an appendix written by another.

(3) The object of the book—to give a history of the conquest and partition of the land.

I. Preparatory to the Conquest. Chaps. 1-5.

1. *Preparation of Rations.* 1:10-11.
2. *Charge to Reubenites, Gadites, and half tribe of Manasseh.* 1:12-18.
3. *Spies Sent to Jericho.* chap. 2.
4. *The Passage of the Jordan.*
   (1) The command of the officers to the people. 3:2-4.
   (2) Joshua to the people, v. 5; to the priests, v. 6.
   (3) The Lord to Joshua. vs. 7-8.
   (4) Joshua to the "Children of Israel." vs. 9-13.
   (5) The miraculous division of the waters of the Jordan and passage of Israel according to God's word. vs. 14-17.
   (6) The memorial of the great event. 4:1-24.
   (7) The effect of this miracle upon the inhabitants of the land. 5:1.
5. *The Observance of the Two Sacraments—Circumcision and Passover.* 5:2-12.
6. *Joshua's Interview with the Captain of the Host of the Lord.* 5:13-15 and 14:1-5.

II. The Conquest. Chaps. 6-12.

The conquest of the land was accomplished in three principal campaigns—the Central, Southern, and Northern Campaigns.

1. *The Central Campaign.*
   (1) The capture of Jericho. 6:6-21. The exception of Rahab. vs. 22-25. The charge of Joshua concerning the spoil. vs. 18-19. The curse upon the builder of Jericho. v. 26.

THIRD PERIOD. 161

(2) *The Capture of Ai.*
   (a) First attack. 7 : 26. The cause of the failure. vs. 7–15. The removal of the cause. vs. 16–26.
   (b) The second attack. 8 : 1–29.
(3) The altar and reading the law. 8 : 30–35.
(4) The Gibeonites. 9 : 3–27.

2. *The Southern Campaign.*
  (1) The alliance of the five kings for the purpose of chastising the Gibeonites and opposing Joshua. 10 : 1–5.
  (2) The Gibeonites send messengers to Joshua at the fortified camp at Gilgal. v. 6.
  (3) The great battle of Beth-horon.
    (a) Joshua's night march. v. 9.
    (b) The slaughter. v. 10.
    (c) The great stones from heaven. v. 11.
    (d) Sun and moon stand still. 12–14.
    (e) The execution of the five kings. 16–27.
    (f) Importance of this victory.
  (4) Additional conquests during this campaign. 10 : 28–43.

3. *The Northern Campaign.*
  (1) The alliance headed by Jabin in the north. 11 : 1–5.
  (2) Joshua by a forced march surprises them. v. 7.
  (3) The Lord delivered them into the hand of Israel. v. 8.
  (4) The result. 8–9.
  (5) Additional conquests during this campaign.

4. *Summary of the Conquests.*
  (1) East of the Jordan. 12 : 1–6.
  (2) In the three campaigns of Joshua west of the Jordan. 11 : 21–23 ; 12 : 7–24.

III. The Partition of the Land.
Chaps. 13-21.
1. The two and a half tribes east of the Jordan. 13 : 8-31; cf. Num. 32 : 1-38.
2. Judah, Ephraim, and Manasseh (west).
    (1) Judah. Chap. 15.
    (2) Ephraim. 16 : 5-10.
    (3) Manasseh. 17 : 1-13.
3. *The Seven Remaining Tribes.*
    (1) Appointment of three men from each tribe to make the division. 18 : 3-9.
    (2) Lots cast for them. 18 : 10.
4. *The Cities of Refuge.* Chap. 20.
5. *Cities Assigned to the Levites.* Chap. 21.
6. *The Tribes East of Jordan Sent Home.* Chap. 22.

IV. The Old Age and Death of Joshua.
Chaps. 23-24.

These chapters transmit two discourses of Joshua to the assembled people of Israel, both of which meetings and addresses must have been near the close of his life.

1. *First Discourse.* Chap. 23. Analyze.
2. *Final Gathering of Israel at Shechem, and Joshua's Closing Discourse.* Analyze.
3. *Character of Joshua.*

V. Supplementary to the Conquest.
Judges, chaps. 1, 17, 18.
1. *The Campaign of Judah and Simeon.* Judges 1 : 1-8.
2. *The Campaign of Caleb and Othniel.* 1 : 12-15.
3. *The Campaign of Joseph.* 1 : 22-26.
4. *The Campaign of Dan.* Chaps. 17-18.

VI. The Extirpation of the Canaanites. (Humphrey.)

First. What was the divine command? Deut. 20:16-18; Ex. 23:32; Ex. 34:10-17; Deut. 7:1-7. All showing that God required the Hebrews—

(1) To make no treaty with the Canaanites.
(2) Not to intermarry with them.
(3) To destroy them utterly, root and branch —the command being explicit, peremptory, and universal.
(4) This lest they should corrupt the Hebrews, especially as to idolatry. Ex. 23:33; 34:12.

Second. The difficulty. How are we to reconcile this with the goodness and mercy and general character of God.

Third. The solution commonly received by the church since Augustine.

1. *The Canaanites Exterminated in Punishment of Their Iniquity.* Proof:

    (1) In Gen. 15:16 we have the reason given why the Israelites could not yet take the land.
    (2) Lev. 18 describes the most revolting and disgusting crimes committed by the Canaanites. Lev. 18:24; Deut. 12:30-31.
    (3) God gave them time (about 500 years) for repentance. In Melchizedek and the patriarchs he had given them wonderful examples of piety. They had heard also of his dealings in Egypt and at the Red Sea; and he waited yet forty years more. Josh. 2:10.

2. *The Israelites were Simply the Instruments for Executing God's Judgments on the Heathen.* If God had employed plagues, earthquakes, etc.,

we would have heard no complaints. But has not God a right to choose his instruments? He employs various instrumentalities, plagues, famines, angels, and men. The Hebrews did not act under the promptings of their own heart. Their case is analogous to a sheriff executing the sentence of the law on a criminal.

3. *This Commission was Authenticated by Miracles.* This a part of the significance of the three great miracles. The sum is that God determined to destroy the heathen for their iniquities, and to employ the Hebrews for executing his divine justice.

4. *Important Purposes Answered by Employing the Hebrews as the Ministers of Justice.*

(1) Adapted to awaken a horror of idolatry—a lesson much needed by them. Nothing is so well suited to give a man a horror of murder as to be compelled to execute the sentence of the law on the criminal.

(2) It served to bring the heathen idols into contempt. Ex. 34:13. They saw the gods of the heathen had no power to protect them.

(3) It was to warn them against imitating the heathen. They were likely to think of what would befall them in such a case. Deut. 12:29; 18:63; Lev. 18:24-28.

REVIEW CHART OF THE THIRD PERIOD.

OUTLINE OF PERIOD.

SEC. 1. The Tenth Plague.
    I. The Plague.
    II. The Passover.
    III. The Exodus.
SEC. 2. Pharaoh Manephtah.
SEC. 3. The Route Chosen.
SEC. 4. The Cloudy Pillar.
SEC. 5. From Succoth to Sinai.
    I. The Red Sea.
    II. Marah.
    III. Wilderness of Sin.
    IV. Meisboh.
    V. Smiting of Amalek.
    VI. Jethro's Visit.
SEC. 6. The Sinaitic Covenant.
    I. The Covenant Described.
    II. The Moral Law.
    III. The Ceremonial Law.
    IV. The Civil Law.
SEC. 7. Other Events at Sinai.
SEC. 8. From Sinai to the Death of Moses.
    Introduction:
    I. From Sinai to Kadesh-Barnea.
    II. Kadesh-Barnea.
    III. From Kadesh to Arnon.
    IV. The Conquests East of the Jordan.
    V. Deuteronomy.
SEC. 9. The Conquest of Canaan.
    Introduction:
    I. Preparatory to the Conquest.
    II. The Conquest.
    III. The Partition of the Land.
    IV. Old Age and Death of Joshua.
    V. Supplementary to the Conquest.
    VI. The Extirpation of the Canaanites.

QUESTIONS ON THE PERIOD.   TOPICS FOR SPECIAL STUDY.

3. What were the uses and religious significance of the Cloudy Pillar?
4. Analyze the Song of Moses after the passage of the Red Sea.
5. What were the leading events between the Red Sea and Sinai?
6. What were the principal features of the Sinaitic Covenant?
7. Why was the Law of God given in the form of a Covenant?
8. What was the significance of the circumstances attending the giving of the Covenant?
9. What are the great moral principles underlying the Decalogue?
10. What was the great purpose of the Ceremonial Law?
11. What were the principal features of the Civil Law?
12. Mention the most important points in the history of the golden calf and explain their significance.
13. How and why was Aaron's call to the Priesthood vindicated?
14. Relate what occurred at Kadesh-Barnea and show its significance.
15. What territory and people were conquered east of the Jordan?
16. What were the great features in the preparation for the conquest of Western Palestine?
17. What territory and people conquered West of the Jordan?
18. The extirpation of the Canaanites—the problem and its solution?
19. What was God's purpose in settling his people in Palestine?

4. The Law of God.
5. Moral and Positive Commands.
6. The Sabbath and Judaism.
7. The Gospel and the Ceremonial Law.
8. The Blood.
9. The Typology of Scripture.
10. Prophecies of Balaam.
11. Battle of Beth-horon.
12. The characters of Moses, Aaron, and Joshua.
13. Why was Palestine chosen to be the home of the chosen people?
14. God and his Church.
15. The progress in the Divine revelations during this Period.

FOURTH PERIOD.

JUDGES.

FROM SETTLEMENT IN CANAAN TO KINGDOM,
450 YEARS. (ACTS 13 : 20.)

Introduction.

OUTLINE OF INTRODUCTION.

I. **Political Condition of Israel after Death of Joshua.**
Stanley's Hist. of Jewish Ch., Lect. 13.
Geikie, Hours, chap. 14.
Butler's Bible Work.

II. **The Moral Condition of the Hebrews at the Death of Joshua.**
Humphrey, Ms. Notes of Lects.
Other references as above.

III. **The Fatal Act of Disobedience.**
Same references as above.

IV. **The Record of the Period.**
Barrow, Companion to Bible, p. 245.
Other references same as above.

V. **Plan of the History of the Period.**
Same references.

NOTES.

I. Political Condition of Israel at the Death of Joshua.

1. "'In those days there was no King in Israel,' but every man 'did that which was right in his own eyes.' 'In those days there was no King in Israel.' 'It came to pass there was no King in Israel.' 'In those days there was no King in Israel.' 'Every man did that which was right in his own eyes.' This sentence, thus frequently and earnestly repeated, is the keynote of the whole book."—*Stanley.* Hence this period "furnishes a striking picture of the disorders and dangers which prevailed in a republic without a magistracy, where the highways were unoccupied and the travelers walked through by-ways, where few prophets arose to control the people, and 'every one did that which was right in his own eyes.'"—*B. B. Wk.*

2. *The Outward Relations of the Country.* "The conquest was over, but the upheaving of the conquered population still continued. The ancient inhabitants, like the Saxons under the Normans, still retained their hold on large tracts, or on important positions, throughout the country. The neighboring powers still looked on the newcomers as an easy prey to incursion and devastation, if not to actual subjugation."—*Stanley.*

II. The Moral Condition of the Hebrews at the Death of Joshua.

This better than at any time before or after. More godly and brave. Proof:

(1) Testimony of Joshua. Josh. 23 : 8.
(2) Their covenant. Josh. 24: 16–25.
(3) Their zeal for the law. Josh. 22.
(4) Their conduct throughout the conquest—brave, obedient, loyal.

III. **Their Fatal Act of Disobedience—Failure to Drive Out the Heathen. They Disobeyed:**
(1) In allowing the heathen to remain in the land. Judges 1 : 21–34.
(2) In making treaties with them.
(3) In intermarrying with them. Judges 3 : 5–6.
(4) As to idolatry. 2 : 11–13.
These results vindicate the original command of God. Deut. 18 : 20; Ex. 23 : 31–32. Hence Judges 2 : 1–5.

IV. **The Record of the Period.**
1. *History of the Judges from Othniel to Samson.* Chaps 1–16.
2. *An Appendix Containing a History of Events immediately after the Death of Joshua.* Chaps. 17, 21. (Already considered.)
3. *The History of the Last Two Judges, Eli and Samuel.* 1 Samuel, chaps. 1, 8.
4. *The Episode.* Book of Ruth.

V. **Plan of the History of the Period. Judges 2: 11-19.**
1. *Their Sin.* vs. 11–13.
2. *Their Punishment.* vs. 14–15.
3. *Their Repentance.* vs. 15–18.
4. *Deliverer Raised Up.* v. 16.
5. *After the Death of the Judge they Returned again to Idolatry.* v. 19. Thus they lived for 450 years, repeating over and over again this history. This the key to the period.

SECTION 1. THE SIX PRINCIPAL OPPRESSIONS AND THE JUDGES.

OUTLINE.

I. **The Mesopotamian—Othniel the Judge.**
Price, Syllabus, O. T. Hist.
Hurlbut, Manual Bib. Geog.
Butler's Bible Work.
Stanley's History of the Jewish Church.

II. **The Moabite—Ehud the Judge.**
Same references.

III. **The Canaanite—Deborah the Judge.**
Same references.

IV. **The Midianite—Gideon the Judge.**
Same references.

V. **The Ammonite—Jephthah the Judge.**
Same references.

VI. **The Philistine—Samson, Eli, and Samuel, Judges.**
Same references.

NOTES.

I. **The Mesopotamian Oppression. 3: 7-11. (See plan of history.)**
 1. *The Oppression.* Why? By whom? How long?
 2. *Deliverance.* When? Judge? Length of rest?

II. **The Moabite Oppression. vs. 12-30. Verify plan of history.**
 1. *The Oppression.* Describe.
 2. *Deliverance.* Describe.

III. **The Canaanite Oppression. Chaps. 4, 5. Verify plan of history.**
1. *The Oppression.* 4:1-3. Describe.
2. *The Deliverance* The history of this deliverance of special interest. Study specially—
    (1) The Judge—Deborah; her character, office, and work.
    (2) The battle; the two armies; the battle-ground; the storm; the death of Sisera; the victory.
    (3) The song of Deborah. Analyze.

IV. **Midianite Oppression. Chaps. 6, 8.**
1. *The Oppression.* 6:1-6.
2. *The Prophet.* 6:7-10.
3. *The Deliverance.*
    (1) Call of Gideon. 6:11-24.
    (2) Preparation of Gideon. vs. 26-40.
    (3) Gideon's army; size at first; after first reduction; after second reduction. 7:1-8.
    (4) The battle and victory. vs. 9-25.
    (5) After the victory. Ephraim 8:1-3. Succoth, Zebah, and Zalmunna. Israel's offer to Gideon. The snare unto Gideon v. 27. Rest forty years.

V. **Ammonite Oppression. Chaps. 10: 6-18; 11: 1-40: 12: 1-7.**
1. *The Oppression.* 10:6-18. Note the points in these verses.
2. *Deliverance.* Note in the history.
    (1) Jephthah. 15:1-11.
    (2) Jephthah and Ammon. vs. 12-28.
    (3) Jephthah's vow. 30-31.
    (4) The victory. 32-33.
    (5) The fulfillment of his vow. 34-40.
    (6) Jephthah and Ephraim. 12:1-6.

VI. The Philistine Oppression. Chaps. 13-16.

1. *The Oppression.* 13-1.
2. *Samson.* Chap. 13 : 2 to Chap. 17.
    (1) History of his birth. 13 : 2–24. The child was to be a Nazarite unto God from his birth unto his death. v. 7. See Num. 6 : 1–21. This the first recorded instance of this vow being carried out.
    (2) Samson's first exploit. Chap. 14.
    (3) Destroys the corn of the Philistines. 15: 1-6.
    (4) Samson at Lehi. 15 : 9–20.
    (5) Samson at Gaza. 16 : 1–3.
    (6) Samson and Delilah. 16 : 4–22.
    (7) Destruction of the house of Dagon, and his own death. 16 : 23–31.
3. *The Character of Samson.* To realize such a character as that of Samson we must restore, in imagination, the circumstances of his times. How great a heart must that have been which dared to stand out alone against a tyranny that crushed and cursed even the strong and warlike tribe of Judah till they consented to thrust him down at the bidding of their masters and deliver him—the one patriot of the land—into the hands of the common enemy. . . . . Nor is his rude but unchanging fidelity to Jehovah as his God less touching. In spite of his being apparently deserted by Him, and though the enemy boasted that Dagon had proved himself a greater god by victory over Jehovah's champion, Samson held fast his faith. His countrymen had turned to idols, but he, in his rough way, clung to the God of his fathers."—*Geikie.*

SECTION 2. ABIMELECH.

CHAP. 9.

Abimelech was an usurper and not worthy to be classed with the Judges appointed of God. Yet a long chapter devoted to his history, from which we learn:
1. *Who he was.* 9:1.
2. *The Conspiracy by which he Succeeded in Slaying all his Brethren except Jotham.* vs. 2-5.
3. *Made King by the Men of Shechem.* v. 6.
4. *Jotham's Parable and Address.* vs. 7-21. This the first recorded parable.
5. *Abimelech's Three Years' Reign.* Describe, mentioning the events.
6. *His Death.* Describe. 50-57.

SECTION 3. THE EPISODE.

BOOK OF RUTH.

Introduction.
1. *Time.* " When the judges judged."
2. *The Picture here given of the Times—peaceful, orderly observance of the Mosaic Institutes.* "It is one of those quiet corners in history which are the green spots of time, and which appear to become greener and greener as they recede into the distance."—*Stanley.*
3. *Character and Contents.* "In this book we have a glimpse into the domestic life of Israel with its anxieties, sorrows, and sweetness. Women and children, honest work and homely talk;

deaths, births, and marriages; loves, memories, and prayers are all here. Human kindness, filial piety, affectionate constancy, uncomplaining toil, true chastity, sweet patience, strong faith, noble generosity, simple piety—are all here, and they are all observed by God and are shown to be pleasing to him, who rewards them in due time.—*Butler's Bible Work.*

DIVISIONS.

I. Elimelech and Naomi and their two Sons in Moab.
1. *Why did they go to Moab?* 1: 1–2.
2. *Death of Elimelech.* v. 3.
3. *Marriage of the two Sons.* v. 4.
4. *Death of the Sons, Mahlon and Chilion.* v. 5.

II. Naomi's Return to Bethlehem.
1. *Her Address to her two Daughters-in-law when she determines to Return.* 1: 7–5 and 11–13.
2. *Their Reply—Orpah—Ruth.* 14–17.
3. *Naomi and Ruth Return to Bethlehem.* vs. 19–22.

III. Ruth Gleans in the Field of Boaz.
1. *Boaz.* Chap. 2.
2. *Gleaning—Connection with Mosaic Institutes.*
3. *Treatment Received from Boaz.*

IV. Ruth Makes herself Known to Boaz. Chap. 3.
1. *The Law of Levirate Marriage.* 3: 11–14; cf. Deut. 25: 5–10.
2. *Boaz Acknowledges the Law and Promises to act Accordingly.*
3. *Ruth's Report to Naomi.*

V. **The Marriage of Boaz and Ruth.**
1. *The Transaction in the Gate.* 4: 1-12.
2. *The Marriage.* v. 13.

Conclusion—The Purpose of the Book.
1. *To preserve the Genealogy of David.*
2. *To preserve the Genealogy of our Lord.*
3. *To present a Picture of the Times.*

SECTION 4. ELI.

OUTLINE.

I. **The Condition of the Country in the Time of Eli.**
Geikie, Hours, chap. 2; O. T. Characters, Eli.
Stanley, Hist. Jewish Ch.

II. **History of Eli.**
Price, Syllabus O. T. Hist.
Bible Dict.
Butler's Bible Work.
Other references as above.

III. **The Battle of Aphek.**
Same references.

IV. **The Fall of Shiloh.**
Same references.

V. **Return of the Ark.**
Same references.

NOTES.

I. **The Condition of the Country in the Time of Eli.**
1. *The Political Condition. Israel Suffering under the Philistine Oppression.* " In Eli's time things

had come, apparently, to the worst, for Samson's heroic efforts had done nothing to stem the progress of Philistine conquest; and it was clear that unless a great deliverance was, ere long, effected, the degradation would be complete, and perhaps permanent."—*Geikie.*

2. *The Moral and Religious Condition—Exceedingly Ungodly.* "Constant intermarriages with the heathen still continued, and had introduced a low morality that sapped the character of the nation even in its priesthood."—*Geikie.*

II. History of Eli.

1. *His Lineage.* Of the line of Ithamar, Aaron's younger son. Lev. 10:12; cf. 1 Kings 2:27 with 2 Sam'l 8:17; 1 Chr. 24:3. Of his early history or how he came into the priesthood nothing is known.

2. *His Offices.* He was both priest and judge. 1 Sam'l 1:9; 4:18.

3. *Interview with Hannah.* 1 Sam'l 1:9-17. This the first appearance of Eli in the history.

4. *Eli and his Sons.* 1 Sam'l 2:12-17 and 22-25.
    (1) The sins of his sons. "Stooping to the level of the debased idolatry around, they had taken part in the impurities that defiled the neighborhood of the tabernacle, and had thus brought discredit on the worship of Jehovah among the few who still clung to the pure faith of their fathers. Nor was this all. The duties of the sanctuary were treated by them with insolent, overbearing disrespect. The very offerings were rudely seized for their own tables, and the sacred office, as a whole, used

only for the gratification of their unbridled self-indulgence."—*Geikie.*
(2) Eli rebukes them in vain. vs. 23-25.
5. *The Message of the Man of God to Eli.* 2:27-36.
(1) Eli's sin. v. 29.
(2) The punishment. 30-36.
6. *Eli and Samuel.*
(1) Taken to Eli and consecrated to the Lord while a child. 1:24-28.
(2) Early association with Eli. 2:11-18.
(3) Vision and message to Eli. 3:1-18. Eli's answer. v. 18.

III. The Battle of Aphek. Chap. 4.

1. *The Battle-ground—Aphek.*
2. *The First Battle.* v. 2.
3. *The Ark Brought by Hophni and Phinehas to the Camp.* Why? Effect upon Israel—upon Philistines. vs. 3-9.
4. *The Second Battle and Results.* vs. 10-13.
5. *The News Carried to Eli.* His death. Judged Israel forty years. vs. 13-18.

IV. The Fall of Shiloh.

1. *Location.* Judges 21:19.
2. *Importance.* The religious capital of the nation. The tabernacle was there, and for centuries the national holy place of Israel. "Thither the faithful had come year after year for the great feast, and to pour out their burdened hearts, like Hannah, before God."—*Geikie.*
3. *Its Overthrow.* Ps. 78:60-67; Judges 7:12, 14.
4. *Removal of the Tabernacle.* 1 Sam. 21:1; 7:1; 2 Chron. 1:3-5. "The tabernacle under

which the ark had rested, was carried off, first, to Nob and then to Gibeon."—*Stanley.*

V. Return of the Ark. Chaps. 5, 6, and 7 : 1-2.
  1. *The Ark at Ashdod.* Results? 5 : 1–9.
  2. *At Ekron.* Results? 10–12.
  3. *The Ark Returned.* Why? How? To what place? 6 : 1–12.
  4. *The Ark at Beth-Shemesh.* Offering. Men smitten. vs. 13–19.
  5. *At Kirjath-jearim.* 7 : 1–2.

SECTION 5. SAMUEL.

OUTLINE.

I. Early Life.
  Geikie, Hours, and O. T. Characters.
  Price, Syllabus O. T. Hist.
  Butler's Bible Work.
  Stanley, Hist. Jewish Church.
  Blaikie, Manual.

II. Samuel as Judge.
  Same references.

III. Samuel under a King.
  Same references.

IV. Samuel's Character and Place in History.
  Geikie, O. T. Characters.
  Butler's Bible Work.

NOTES.

I. Early Life.

1. *Given in Answer to Prayer.* 1 Sam. 1: 10-13. Note the earnestness of this prayer—that she here makes a vow unto God—and that this was silent prayer. At his birth she called him Samuel, that is, Asked of God. 1: 20.

2. *Consecrated to God in Early Childhood even as the Mother had Vowed.* 1: 24-28.

3. *Hannah's Song at Samuel's Formal Consecration.* 2: 1-10. Analyze. " Her song of thanksgiving is the first hymn, properly so-called, the direct model of the first Christian hymn of the 'Magnificat,' the first outpouring of individual as distinct from national devotion, the first indication of the greatness of the anointed king, whether in the divine or human sense."— *Stanley.*

4. *His Ministry with Eli.* 2: 18-19.

5. *The first Divine Revelation made to Samuel.* 3: 1-18. Significance? Established to be a prophet. vs. 20-21. For twenty years the record is silent concerning Samuel.

II. Samuel as Judge.

1. *Gathers all Israel to Mizpah.*
   (1) The preparation for the general gathering. 7: 2-4. During the twenty years concerning which the record is silent Samuel had doubtless been actively engaged along the line indicated by these verses. " The long-haired prophet, in his mantle, who for so many years had been moving hither and

thither among the people, seeking to stir them to new zeal for the faith of their fathers, had at last fairly roused them. They had come to feel the truth of his words, that a return to Jehovah was their only, but certain, hope of deliverance from the yoke of the Philistines."—*Geikie.*

(2) The solemn convocation at Mizpah. vs. 5–10. (*a*) The repentance of the people. v. 6. "Amid symbolical acts and the observance of a universal fast, Israel confessed its past sin and once more joined itself to the God of its fathers." (*b*) Samuel's prayer for Israel. vs. 5, 8, 9.

(3) The battle. The news of the assembly at Mizpah reached the Philistines and led them to attack Israel. But because Jehovah was now on Israel's side the Philistines suffered a great defeat. vs. 10–11. The fruit of the victory. 13–14. The Ebenezer stone. v. 12.

2. Samuel discharges the duties of judge. 7: 15–17. After the great victory at Ebenezer "he appeared no more in the field, but confined himself to making circuits through the land, judging the various districts."

3. *Samuel's Sons.* He had made them his assistants in his work. But they proved unworthy. 8: 1–5.

4. *The People Demand a King.* 8: 4–22.
  (1) The demand made. 4–5.
  (2) Samuel displeased, but seeks counsel from God. v. 6.
  (3) The Lord's answer. vs. 7–9.
  (4) Samuel delivers God's answer to the people

and tells them what they might expect from a king. vs. 10–22.

5. *Samuel Anoints Saul.* Chaps. 9–10.
  (1) The providence which led Saul to the city where Samuel was. 9:1–14.
  (2) God's revelation to Samuel. 9:15–17.
  (3) Samuel entertains Saul and anoints him. 9:18–27 and 10:1.
  (4) Samuel foretells Saul the incidents of his return journey and arranges another meeting at Gilgal. 10:2–8.
  (5) Saul among the Prophets. 10:9–13.

6. *The Selection of Saul as King at Mizpah.* In this election Samuel the ruling spirit.
  (1) He calls the assembly. 10:17.
  (2) Delivers God's message. 18–19.
  (3) Presides and prescribes the method of the election. vs. 19–21.
  (4) Presents Saul to the people. v. 24.
  (5) Declares the manner of the kingdom and writes it in a book—then dismisses the people. 25, 26.

7. *The Kingdom Formally Inaugurated at Gilgal.* 11:14–15; chap. 12.
  (1) Samuel convenes the assembly. 11:14.
  (2) Saul formally inducted into office. 11:15.
  (3) Samuel's farewell address in retiring from his office as judge. Chap. 12. Analyze.

III. Samuel under a King.

1. *Rebukes Saul.* 13:8–15.
2. *Samuel Announces to Saul his Rejection as King.*
  (1) The commission he received from God. 15:1–3.
  (2) Saul's disobedience. 15:4–9.

(3) Samuel to Saul. vs. 17–23. Although Saul sought pardon, yet Samuel was firm. 24–31.
3. *Samuel Completes the Work of Judgment.* vs. 32–33.
4. *Samuel Mourns for Saul.* vs. 34–35.
5. *Samuel Sent to Annoint David King.* 16:1–13. Describe.
6. *Samuel at Ramah.* 16:13; 19:18–22; 25:1.
   (1) Ramah his home. Locate.
   (2) His influence in Israel. 19:18–22.
   (3) His death. 25:1.

IV. Samuel's Character and Place in History.

1. *His Character.* "The imposing greatness of Samuel's character is seen in the results of his work. He found his people in the deepest national degradation, politically and religiously, and left them on the eve of the most splendid era in their history—the age of their widest dominion as a nation and their greatest glory as worshipers of Jehovah."—*Geikie.*

   "His sublime figure stands out in the pages of Holy Writ as a signal example of faith, of patience, of integrity, of self-sacrifice, through a long and trying career, fulfilling the promise of those early days in Shiloh when he grew on and was in favor with the Lord and with man." —*B. B. Wk.*

2 *His Place in History.* He was the last of the Judges, and the founder of the kingdom. He was a great deliverer, a great reformer, a great ruler, a great prophet, and the establisher of the monarchy. He lived at one of the great epochs in Jewish history, and was God's instrument in making the epoch.

SECTION 6. THE AGE OF SAMUEL AND THE PROPHETIC OFFICE.

OUTLINE.

I. **By What Events Was this Age Distinguished?**
   Humphrey, Ms. Notes of Lects.
   Stanley, Hist. of Jewish Church.

II. **The Prophetic Office.**
   Same references.

III. **The Nature of the Prophetic Inspiration.**
   Same references.

IV. **Training and Education of the Prophets.**
   Same references.

V. **In What Manner Were the Prophecies Uttered?**
   Same references.

VI. **The Prophetic Eras.**
   Same references.

NOTES.

I. **By What Events Was this Age Distinguished?**

1. *The Close of the Period of the Judges.* In Samuel the judges ceased and a new form of government was introduced.

2. *The Victory Over the Philistines.* The Philistine oppression had lasted forty years—the most disastrous of the servitudes. It was divided into three periods: (1) Under Samson, characterized by his single-handed exploits. He was the army of the country. (2) Under Eli,

characterized by an attempt to use the ark of God superstitiously. (3) Under Samuel, characterized by the reformation of the people, return of God's favor and the consequent defeat of the Philistines.

3. *The Introduction of Two New Elements into the Hebrew State, Prophets and Kings.* Strictly speaking, the prophetic element existed before, but it now received a fresh impulse.

II. The Prophetic Office.

In general terms, the prophet is one who declares to man the will of God by divine inspiration. Prediction only one function of his office. It is also his to reveal the hidden past and present. Danl., chap. 2; 1 Kings 5:20; John 4:19.

III. The Nature of the Prophetic Inspiration.

1. *It Was Plenary.* 2 Tim. 3:16; 2 Pet. 1:21.
2. *The Form of Revelation Various.* Heb. 1:1. Sometimes in visions. Isa. 6:1. Hence the name seer. Sometimes by dreams, voices, Urim and Thummim.

IV. Training and Education of the Prophets.

The subject in great obscurity. There were schools of the prophets. 2 Kings 2:3, 5, 7, 15. See also 1 Saml. 19:20. "The schools of the prophets were evidently very important and much blessed institutions. Young men, chiefly Levites, were trained in these schools to explain the law of God to his people and to enforce its claims."—*Blaikie.*

V. In What Manner Were the Prophecies Uttered?

1. *Orally from Moses to Uzziah*—*e. g., Nathan, Elijah, Elisha.*

2. *In Writing*—*e. g., Ezekiel.* Ez. chaps. 40–48.
3. *Orally and then Committed to Writing.* Probably Isaiah.
4. *By Symbolical Action.* Jer. 13 : 1–10; Acts 21 : 11.

VI. The Prophetic Eras.

1. *The Prophetic Gift without the Office*—*e. g.,* Jacob, Balaam. Moses an exception to this general statement.
2. *From Samuel to Uzziah.* 800 years. Prophets of action, who left no written report—*e. g.,* Nathan, Elijah.
3. *From Uzziah to Malachi.* Prophets by profession, who left writings.

www.ingramcontent.com/pod-product-compliance
Lightning Source LLC
Chambersburg PA
CBHW020907230426
43666CB00008B/1352